76 WEEK GOETIA

A Goetia Immersion Experience

S. Connolly

Darkerwood Publishing Group LLC.

Darkerwood Publishing Group LLC, Denver, CO

Available In:
eBook
Paperback
Case Wrap Hardcover
Linen Wrap Hardcover
Spiral Bound

Editorial: M. Blackthorne
Cover: S. Connolly
Interior Design by S. Connolly

INSTRUCTIONS

Instructions for this Home Study Goetia
Immersion

First, you can skip around and work with the
Daemons you wish. You can also use this book as
inspiration for your own personal path work.
Otherwise, you can use this book to spend 76 weeks
working with the Goetia spirits. One Daemon a
week (the four elementals at the end).

This is as much a book of pathworking and high
magick as it can be a book of low magick. Its
limitations are in the eye of the beholder.

This is also an advanced course as you are
expected to already know how to do the following
and no instruction on this is provided in this text:

Prerequisites: An understanding how to perform
ritual as this book expects you to create your own
rituals/spells. It assumes you already understand
and know how to do Invocation or Evocation (as
your personal practice dictates). It expects you are
already fluent in basic spirit communication
techniques and have a working knowledge and
understanding of meditation. It also assumes you
have a basic, functional understanding of magick. If

you're missing any of those, please brush up on those areas of study and return to this book when you have enough experience to do this immersion.

While I made some effort for formatting consistency, you may notice heading variations in weeks 1-30 and minor formatting variations week to week. In one week, I might use bullet points. The next week I might use a numbered list. One week a heading might say Meditation. The next week Meditate. This book is an almost exact replica of the course taught in 2022-2023, though definitely cleaned up for spelling, punctuation, and readability. Each week's lessons were written individually, so variation was inevitable. I saw no reason to make sure each week was exactly like the week before because the premise and instruction is still the same and it does not detract from the content material, which is the more important part of this text. You will notice more consistency in each day's titles after week thirty when I began copy/pasting a standard template for each set of lessons. If I ever write something this monstrous again, I will definitely pay more attention to using templates from the start.

YOU WILL NEED

1. Several notebooks. You're going to be taking a lot of notes. You might consider *The Goetia Workbook* as one of those notebooks so you can

make notes about each Daemon as you work with them. You can use a single notebook for everything, or you can have separate notebooks for dreams, freewriting, and reflection.

2. About 10-40 minutes a day, depending how much time you'd like to dedicate to this experience.

3. A quiet place to meditate and work ritual. If you don't have a physical space, your astral temple will suffice.

4. See below for suggested supplies. But, for what it's worth, you can go without supplies.

I suggest reading this book at least once or twice before jumping in. Reading the book through will give you an idea of the time you need and supplies you may want to get if you are practicing in a physical space. I recommend a ton of incense sticks and a variety of colored small charm candles or tealights along with a divination device or two. You'll also need pen and paper, and a fire safe bowl. But again, this course can be done without supplies at all.

The beauty of having this course in book form is that you can skip weeks, start whenever you like, or just pick and choose the exercises you'd like to try when you want to try it. Each week is a wonderful way to introduce yourself to each Goetic spirit individually.

Please note that this course was originally

written for Daemonolaters. We don't command, enslave, or torture spirits. We work WITH them respectfully. If you prefer traditional ceremonial magick methods, that's your business. No judgment. Just modify the parts you disagree with as needed.

I'd also like to tell you why I choose the particular sigil set in this book to work with. I could have hired an artist to render beautiful artwork. But instead, I like the hand drawn, raw look of these sigils. Far too often books of magick have perfectly rendered seals by artists, and this can make working magicians who aren't artists feel like they need perfection. I want to normalize that magicians don't have to be artistically inclined to work with sigils. I want your sigils to be imperfect and your magick to be messy. Because that's how it is in the real world. Learn to let go of your need for perfection. The Daemonic is not nearly as uptight and petty as we humans are, certainly. They won't get "angry" with you if you don't have the right color candle, or you invoke them on a Tuesday instead of a Thursday. Or if you have the wrong altar cloth.

That said, if you BELIEVE they're petty and quick to anger – you will create a self-fulfilled prophecy and can self-destruct. The Daemonic doesn't need to help you. You'll do it all by yourself. What you believe has power. If you learn nothing else about yourself or the Daemons from this immersion – I hope you learn that. I mean, obviously I hope you take a lot more away from this course than that but do keep the above in mind as you move forward.

THE SCHEDULE

Trust me when I say that getting through all seventy-two of the Goetic spirits, plus the four elementals, takes a lot of discipline and having discipline is a lot easier if you have a schedule. Feel free to revise the schedule to work for you but have a schedule so you won't fall off the wagon.

MONDAYS: Meditation on the Daemon, its purposes, and its sigil.

TUESDAYS: Freewriting Exercise. You use the writing prompts provided to journal your thoughts.

WEDNESDAY: Dreamwork. Place the sigil beneath your pillow, mattress, or bed.

THURSDAY: Invocation/Evocation #1

FRIDAY: Invocation/Evocation #2

SATURDAY: Create a Spell or Ritual with the Daemon (aka Daemonic Arts & Crafts)
SUNDAY: Reflection, Rest, Meditation, Plan (for the

coming week)

NOTES: Some exercises will have various options for you to choose. Choose what you're most comfortable with. You will also notice the first few weeks will seem moderately repetitive. This is to get you into a routine. That said, the exercises start going deeper and change as you go on. So, if you find yourself getting bored, you're welcome to modify. You'll also notice that I ask you a lot of questions to get you thinking about the work you're doing. Answer these questions in your journal.

Don't let yourself get overwhelmed.

Every time I do this class virtually, I end up losing students as the weeks go on. Most of them citing the fact that they just don't have the time to keep up.

I totally get this, and I also get how overwhelming the immersion can be. Just take it one week at a time. You're going to have weeks where you must miss because something happens. Just make a note of those Daemons and tack them onto the end. Or at least draw their sigil and place it somewhere you can see it for that week. If that's the only thing you manage to do is look at the sigil, or carry the Daemon's seal with you, that's what you do.

Now, take a deep breath, and think of all the things you'll get from completing this immersion, even if you are just drawing the sigil and contemplating it for a week:

1. A deeper understanding of the Goetic spirits both individually and collectively.
2. A deeper understanding of yourself, plus personal edification, and personal enrichment.
3. A deeper understanding of magick.
4. Bragging rights (because let's face it -- it takes a lot of work to work through 76 Daemons. 72 + 4 Elementals)
5. A completed (hopefully) journal detailing your work.

I fully expect at least three-fourths of the people who start this immersion to drop it in the first year. Those who are left standing at the end will deserve their laurels, indeed.

So don't panic, and if you start feeling overwhelmed and life starts kicking your ass and sucking up your free time, remember that it's okay to just draw a sigil and look at it, or to pause and resume as necessary.

More of My Books You May Find Helpful:

- *The Goetia Workbook* - For your personal

notes and ritual considerations for each Daemon.

- *Daemonolatry Goetia* - To learn the basic way to work with the Goetia Daemons ala Daemonolatry style. You can modify this, of course, or work with the spirits via traditional Goetia methods if you're a ceremonial magician. The choice is yours.
- *The Art of Creative Magick* - For creating your own spells and rituals.
- *Lake of Fire* - To learn the Daemonolatry method of ascension practice.
- *Drawing Down Belial* - To hone your divination and spirit communication skills.
- Wortcunning for Daemonolatry - To make your own incenses and oils for the Goetic spirits (and others) if you feel so inclined.

A note about the dates: The dates prescribed to each Daemon in this book for the spirits is based on the work of Crowley and follows Thelema. There are sources for other dates. Golden Dawn has their own set of dates as prescribed by the paper titled *Booke of the Black Serpent*, which was printed at the back of a 1997 version of *The Grimoirium Verum* printed by Trident Books, and Carol Poke Runyon has a different set of dates in his book, *The Book of Solomon's Magick*. So, if you've been curious about the various dates for the Goetic Spirits and wondered why they don't always match book to book or system to system, that is why. People use the decans (of the zodiac of which there are 72, 6 in each of the twelve signs) to break them down differently. Use the dates that work best for you.

WEEK 1: BAEL

KING
Color: Yellow.
Incense: Frankincense.
Metal: Gold.
Planet: Sun
Element: Fire
Enn: *Ayer secore on ca Bael*
Date: March 21- March 30

Original Purposes: Invisibility, primarily.

Author's Notes: Some view Bael as the fire part of Ba'al. He rules over solstices and fire festivals and can bring together friends. He can spark creativity and instruct people in matters of the heart. If you seek him for wealth, let it be in creative wealth or wealth created by creative projects. It is suggested you wear his sigil when invoking him.

Week 1 - Bael - Meditation

Meditate on the sigil of Bael. Think of invisibility (broadly and metaphorically), creativity, inspiration. Be sure to note how the sigil makes you feel. Look it over. What does it evoke in you? What thoughts come to mind as you're focusing on the seal.

Shoot for the following meditation times:

> Beginner: 10 minutes
> Advanced: 20 minutes

Week 1- Bael - Freewrite

In this freewriting exercise, I want you to write down all the ways in which Bael can help you creatively, inspirationally, or to help you keep yourself or your projects out of the limelight (for the moment while you're working on them). Journal about this for 10 minutes (or longer if needed). The point of the exercise is to reflect on how Bael can influence your current situations and help you become better, stronger, more creative etc...

Week 1 – Bael - Dreamwork

Place the seal of Bael beneath your bed, between your mattresses or under your pillow. Before you go to sleep, contemplate the meditation and freewriting exercises you've already done. Lay down and focus on Bael. Recite his enn as you close your eyes. Go to sleep with the intention of communicating with the Daemon. Keep a journal and pen beside your bed so you can write down anything you remember from your dreams immediately upon waking.

How did this exercise go for you? Don't be discouraged if you don't get anything. You'll be repeating this exercise with other Daemons as we move along. You're also welcome to repeat this exercise with Bael for the remainder of the week.

Week 1 – Bael - Invocation #1

Today, I want you to vibrate the enn of Bael and sit in his presence for a few moments. Then I want you to create something inspired by the Daemon. The point of this exercise is to find inspiration. Make notes in your journal. If you feel inspired to create something now, pull out the crafting supplies - it's time for some Daemonic arts and crafts!

More Advanced Students: You may choose to do a

full invocation via constructed ritual space and perform a scrying session.

What did this invocation inspire? How did the Daemonic force feel when you drew it into your space by vibrating the enn?

Week 1 – Bael - Invocation #2

Today I want you to invoke Bael by vibrating the enn, and once the energy in the room chances, simply ask the Daemon for wisdom/advice/clarity on a creative (or invisibility) matter. Just an aside here - if Bael can make things invisible, it stands to reason he can also make visible. What needs to be more visible in your life?

Feel free to do a more formal, full-blown invocation if you so choose.

For more advanced practitioners: Go into ascension and speak with the Daemonic force directly.

Week 1 – Bael - Create a Spell or Ritual

Today, I want you to create a spell or ritual to help you become invisible (or visible). Or you can create a ritual for creative inspiration. A good resource here is *The Art of Creative Magick*. The book can teach you how to create your own spells and rituals.

Week 1 – Bael – Rest/Reflect/Plan/Meditate

Use today to plan your upcoming week, and to either rest or meditate as you need to.

Are there any final reflections you've had about your week-long work with Bael? If so, please write them in your journal today.

WEEK 2: AGARES

DUKE
Color: Green.
Incense: Sandalwood.
Metal: Copper.
Planet: Venus
Element: Earth
Enn: *Rean ganen ayar da Agares*
Date: March 31 – April 10

Original Purpose: Teaches languages, destroys dignities, finds runaways, and causes earthquakes.

Author's Notes: It is said you should wear his sigil after the work in question. Seek Agares for wisdom in friendship and to make your garden grow. He also gives advice on financial matters with regard to projects.

Week 2 - Agares - Meditation

I want you to meditate on the sigil of Agares and consider the following areas: Friendship, advice on projects, and financial matters. Which of those areas could benefit you most right now? This time around I want you take a blank piece of paper and draw the sigil while thinking about these areas, or the area that could most benefit you.

Week 2 – Agares - Freewrite

Today I want you to write down all the ways the Daemon may be able to do to help you become more financially stable, have stronger friendships, or what advice he may be able to give you. Also write down any first impressions of Agares you may have. Any pervading thoughts you keep having in regard to this particular spirit. Or write down any random thoughts that show up, too. You never know how they may be relevant.

Week 2 – Agares - Dreamwork

Repeat the dreamwork exercise for Agares. Place the Daemon's seal beneath your pillow, under the bed, or between your mattresses. Think of all the things you came up with during your meditation and freewriting sessions. Think of the seal. You can repeat the enn as you're falling asleep. Go into the dream with the intent of communicating with the Daemonic and bringing any advice or wisdom into the waking world.

Keep a journal and pen next to the bed so you can immediately write down any dreams or ideas upon waking.

Week 2 – Agares - Invocation #1

Today, I want you to vibrate the enn of Agares and sit in his presence for a few moments. Then I want you to create something inspired by the Daemon. Perhaps it's a magickal artifact, or a sigil to draw friends to you or strengthen your existing friendships. The point of this exercise is to find inspiration. Make notes in your journal. If you feel inspired to create something now, pull out the crafting supplies - it's time for some Daemonic arts and crafts!

What did this invocation inspire? How did the Daemonic force feel when you drew it into your space by vibrating the enn?

Week 2 – Agares - Invocation #2

Today I want you to invoke Agares by vibrating the

enn, and once the energy in the room changes, simply ask the Daemon for wisdom/advice/clarity on friendships, projects, or financial matters. Pay attention to any thoughts or ideas that pop into your head and write them down.

For more advanced practitioners: Go into ascension and speak with the Daemonic force directly.

Week 2 – Agares - Create a Spell or Ritual

Today, I want you to create a spell or ritual to help you in any of the areas you think Agares can help you in. Again, these include friendships, financial matters, and even projects.

If this exercise feels too taxing or advanced for you, you're welcome to just meditate.

Week 2 – Agares – Rest/Reflect/Plan/Meditate

Use today to plan your upcoming week, and to either rest or meditate as you need to.

Are there any final reflections you have about your weeklong work with Agares? If so, please write them in your journal.

WEEK 3: VASSAGO

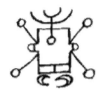

PRINCE
Color: Blue.
Incense: Cedar.
Metal: Tin.
Planet: Jupiter.
Element: Water
Enn: *Keyan vefa jedan tasa Vassago*
Date: April 11 – April 20

Original Purpose: Divination (past and future), to find lost and hidden things.

Author's Notes: Contact Vassago to find out if an enemy has cursed you or is doing something behind your back. Vassago is also good counsel regarding friendship and other interactions with people. He can advise you in negotiations.

Week 3- Vassago - Meditation

I want you to meditate on the sigil of Vassago and consider the following areas: Divination, Friendship, Opportunities. Which of those areas could benefit you most right now? This time around I want you take a blank piece of paper and draw the sigil while thinking about these areas, or the area that could most benefit you.

Week 3- Vassago: Freewrite

In this freewriting exercise, I want you to write down all the ways in which Vassago can help you. Journal about this for 10 minutes (or longer if needed). The point of the exercise is to reflect on how the Daemon can influence your current situations and help you become better, stronger, more creative etc...

Week 3: Vassago - Dreamwork

Place the Daemon's seal beneath your pillow, under the bed, or between your mattresses. Think of all the things you came up with during your meditation and freewriting sessions. Think of the seal. You can repeat the enn as you're falling asleep. Go into the dream with the intent of communicating with the Daemonic and bringing any advice or wisdom into the waking world.
Keep a journal and pen next to the bed so you can

immediately write down any dreams or ideas upon waking.

Week 3 -Vassago- Invocation/Evocation #1

Bring a mirror into the ritual space with you today. I want you to vibrate the enn of Vassago and sit in his presence for a few moments. Perhaps try vibrating the enn a few different ways.

Then I want you to think, "I want to be more [you fill in the blank]." Some ideas: Confident, strong, beautiful, sexy, capable, knowledgeable. You can say this aloud to yourself. Now look into the mirror. Visualize yourself being this thing. See yourself change.

What · did this invocation inspire? How did the Daemonic force feel when you drew it into your space by vibrating the enn?

Week 3 – Vassago - Invocation/Evocation #2

Today I want you to invoke Vassago by vibrating the enn, and once the energy in the room chances, simply ask the Daemon for wisdom/advice/clarity on a matter he can help with.

For more advanced practitioners: Go into ascension and speak with the Daemonic force directly.

Week 3 – Vassago Create a Spell or Ritual

Today, I want you to create a spell or ritual to help you with Divination. Or you can create a ritual for self-transformation.

Alternatively - you may simply perform a divination session using a divination tool of your choice after drawing Vassago into your ritual space. Did this session feel more powerful than without the invocation?

Week 3- Vassago- Rest/Reflect/Plan/Meditate

Use today to plan your upcoming week, and to either rest or meditate as you need to.

Are there any final reflections you'd like to note about your weeklong work with Vassago? Write them in your journal.

WEEK 4: GAMIGIN/SAMIGINA

MARQUIS
Color: Violet
Incense: Jasmine
Metal: Silver
Planet: Moon
Element: Water
Enn: *Esta ta et tasa Gamigin*
Date: April 21 - 30

Original Purpose: Liberal Sciences and Speaking to dead sinners.

Author's Notes: *Also, Samigina.* Necromancy (to speak with any spirits of the dead). Invoke Gamigin to help in creative endeavors. An artist's Daemonic force. Seek Gamigin for inspiration.

Week 4 - Gamigin - Meditation

I want you to meditate on the sigil of Gamigin and consider the following areas: inspiration, creativity, and necromancy. Which of those areas could benefit you most right now? I want you take a blank piece of paper and draw the sigil while thinking about these areas, or the area that could most benefit you. Please note any insights you have during this exercise.

Week 4 – Gamigin - Freewrite

In this freewriting exercise, I want you to write down how you feel about death, or any concerns you've had about a creative endeavor. Journal about this for 10 minutes (or longer if needed). The point of the exercise is to reflect on how the Daemon can influence your current situations and help you become better, stronger, more creative etc...

Week 4 - Gamigin – Dreamwork

You know the drill! Place the Daemon's seal beneath your pillow, under the bed, or between your mattresses (or on your whiteboard above your bed). Think of all the things you came up with during your meditation and freewriting sessions. Think of the seal. You can repeat the enn as you're falling asleep. Go into the dream with the intent of communicating with the Daemonic and bringing any advice or wisdom into the waking world.

Keep a journal and pen next to the bed so you can immediately write down any dreams or ideas upon waking.

Week 4 - Gamigin - Invocation/Evocation #1

Again, you know what's coming. I want you to vibrate the enn of Gamigin and sit in his presence for a few moments. Then I want you to create something inspired by the Daemon. The point of this exercise is to find inspiration. Make notes in your journal. If you feel inspired to create something now, pull out the crafting supplies. Alternatively, you can choose to do a scrying session to speak to the dead (depending on your interest in such things.)

What did this invocation inspire? How did the Daemonic force feel when you drew it into your space by vibrating the enn?

Week 4 - Gamigin - Invocation/Evocation #2

Today I want you to invoke Gamigin by vibrating the enn, and once the energy in the room changes, simply ask the Daemon for wisdom/advice/clarity on any matter.

For more advanced practitioners: Go into ascension and speak with the Daemonic force directly.

These exercises may initially feel like they're a bit repetitive as the exercises are similar for the first part of the course, however, note that repetition will build both consistency and discipline in your practice. We'll expand these exercises as we move further through the immersion.

Week 4 - Gamigin – Create a Spell or Ritual

Today, I want you to create a spell or ritual to help you in working with Gamigin. Listen to your intuition. Think about what it's telling you. Are you inspired to go outdoors? To use a divination device to speak with the dead? A new method you've never tried before? Explore why this is and what it can teach you.

Week 4 – Gamigin - Rest/Reflect/Plan/Meditate

Use today to plan your upcoming week, and to either rest or meditate as you need to.
Are there any final reflections you'd like to note about your weeklong work with Gamigin? If so, please note then in your journal.

I'm also curious as to if you experimented with both Gamigin and the name Samigina if you noticed a difference in energy between the two. If you experimented with the name variants, make a special note about this in your journal.

WEEK 5: MARBAS

PRESIDENT
Color: Orange
Incense: Storax
Metal: Mercury
Planet: Mercury
Element: Air
Enn: Renich Tasa Uberaca Biasa Icar Marbas
Date: May 1-10

Original Purpose: Uncovering secrets, causing and healing illnesses, and mechanical arts.

Author's Notes: Healing and cursing (obviously). Invoke when studying mechanics of any kind including mechanics of the human body (i.e. medicine) to retain and learn more. Invoke Marbas to cause you to see truth in any situation.

Week 5 - Marbas - Meditation

I want you to meditate on the sigil of Marbas and consider the following areas: Healing, revenge, and any feelings which may be standing in the way of your recovery. Which area would most benefit you now?

Week 5 - Marbas - Freewrite

In this freewriting exercise, I want you to write down all the ways in which you may be hindering your own recovery or keeping yourself from letting go of a bad situation. Journal about this for 10 minutes (or longer if needed).

Week 5 - Marbas - Dreamwork

Sleep is when our body repairs itself and relieves our stress, keeping our bodies in good health and soothing our weary psyches.

Even stress and psychological upset can have a negative effect on our bodies and immune systems. Keep this in mind for tonight's work.

As usual, focus on the seal (that you've placed somewhere beneath or above you). You can repeat the enn as you're falling asleep, but this time I want you to go into the dream with the intent of allowing Marbas to heal you in some way. You may also ask for his advice in any area of health. If you can take control of the dream, visualize your body repairing itself. Imagine your stress floating away.

Keep a journal and pen next to the bed so you can

immediately write down any dreams or ideas upon waking.

I am curious if you felt refreshed and well upon waking up or feeling more exhausted than usual.

Week 5 - Marbas - Invocation/Evocation #1

Today, I want you to vibrate the enn of Marbas and sit in his presence for a few moments. You may petition him for healing, ask for answers on health issues, or even petition him to destroy an enemy or ask him how to overcome your foes. He can also help reveal secrets, so keep that in mind when you choose what to do for your first invocation/evocation.
What did this invocation inspire? How did the Daemonic force feel when you drew it into your space by vibrating the enn?

Week 5 - Marbas - Invocation/Evocation #2

You know the drill. Vibrate the enn and draw Marbas into your space. You might consider doing a scrying session, or other divination session in the presence of Marbas today. Maybe search for something missing in your life?

For more advanced practitioners: Go into ascension and speak with the Daemonic force directly.

Week 5 - Marbas - Create a Spell or Ritual

Today, I want you to create a spell or ritual to help you find healing or truth. For those of you who are more poetic, you may choose to write a poem or something in honor of Marbas. For artists, perhaps a talisman of some type.

Week 5- Marbas - Rest/Reflect/Plan/Meditate

Write up your final reflections about your weeklong work with Marbas in your journal.

WEEK 6: VALEFOR

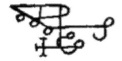

DUKE
Color: Green
Incense: Sandalwood
Metal: Copper
Planet: Venus
Element: Earth
Enn: *Keyman vefa tasa Valefor*
Date: May 11 -20

Original Purpose: Gives good familiars and tempts magicians to steal (apparently).

Author's Notes: Teaches loyalty and the arts of manipulation. Can show you how to charm others and get what you want. Wear Valefor's seal during rituals to invoke, and afterward to manifest the desired results.

Week 6 - Valefor - Meditate

Today I want you to draw the sigil of Valefor. Perhaps even paint it, or sculpt, or carve it. Or even just print it out and add some color using colored pencils. Frame it or hang it somewhere you can see it. Set it front and center. As you draw the sigil, dig deep into yourself and find your confidence and your ability to charm/persuade others with that confidence. Fill the sigil with confidence.

Week 6 - Valefor - Freewrite

Today, I want you to write down all the ways in which Valefor can help you. Journal about this for 10 minutes (or longer if needed). The point of the exercise is to reflect on how the Daemon can influence your current situations and help you become better, stronger, more creative etc...
How many of you have noticed that freewriting helps keep you more focused throughout your day? It's not for everyone. If you can't get down with the freewriting exercises, compose a piece of music or draw something. Or, in the very least, allow yourself to daydream what it would be like with more Valefor influence in your life.

Week 6 - Valefor - Dreamwork

As usual, place the sigil. Before falling asleep, or as you're falling asleep, go into your slumber thinking of a problem you need to solve and your desire for Valefor to help you. What is the result? Did you get any dream imagery that gives you a clue what your course of action should be?
For those advanced in dream-walking: Try taking the Daemon with you to view your situation. What

comes of it?

Week 6 - Valefor - Invocation/Evocation #1

After you invoke Valefor, I want you to attempt to do a divination (scrying, tarot, pendulum) about a problem you'd like to solve or about how to go about getting something you want. Take notes.
For advanced students: Feel free to do a traditional scrying ritual.

Week 6 - Valefor - Invocation/Evocation #2

Today's suggested exercise is to invoke Valefor and ask the Daemon what areas of self-work need to be performed in order to manifest what you desire. Then just listen.

Sometimes Daemons are painfully direct. Other times they're cryptic and give archaic answers that feel like riddles to solve. What kind of answer did you get? Direct or cryptic?

Week 6 - Valefor - Create a Spell or Ritual

Today I want you to formulate a spell or ritual for confidence or glamour utilizing Valefor's energy as a catalyst to the manifestation.

Week 6 - Valefor - Rest/Plan/Meditate

Use today to plan your upcoming week, and to either rest or meditate as you need to.

Are there any final reflections you'd like to note about your weeklong work with Valefor? If so, please write them in your journal. I recommend writing down everything about your experience with the Daemon you're working with. Include things like feelings you get, body sensations, smells, sounds, or visions. Also note whether you feel tired or energetic, thirsty, or warm or cold. And so on. This way you can more easily identify patterns and see how your energy interacts with the Daemonic energy.

WEEK 7 : AMON

MARQUIS
Color: Violet
Incense: Jasmine
Metal: Silver
Planet: Moon
Element: Water
Enn: Avage secore Amon ninan
Date: May 21 – 31

Original Purpose: Predicts the future, knows the past. He can be invoked to cause or reconcile feuds between friends.

Author's Notes: Some see Amon as a fire Daemon to be worshiped at the Summer Solstice. Amon can help bring emotions to a head so that they can be released as usable energy. Amon can help with finding friends.

Week 7 - Amon - Meditate

This week during your meditation, I want you to choose one of the areas Amon excels in, including divination, friendships, and mental well-being. Which of these areas could you use some help or insight into? Feel out Amon's energy. Note any feelings, smells, or sensations.

One thing people often forget about meditation is it's not necessarily about clearing your mind, or even focusing. You'll sometimes find things that have been nagging at you jump into your brain while you're sitting there in the silence. This is okay. Just observe the thoughts (without reacting) and watch them pass, then think of the Daemon again. If a particular thought keeps coming up, perhaps focus that Amon energy toward the thought and see what happens.

Week 7 - Amon – Freewrite

This session is a good time to let out any emotions you may have about anything. Or you can write about a friendship, or where you see yourself 10 years from now. If you are prone to depression or anxiety, write about that. Address it like you're writing a letter to your Daemonic friend (metaphorically speaking), Amon. During your invocation later this week, you might try channeling the Daemon and have him write a response to your letter.

I know - weird, but this is an exercise some of my former students really enjoyed.

Week 7 - Amon - Dreamwork

During this session, ask Amon to show you something in your future. It may work, it may not, but it's worth a try.

Some folks mentioned, with Marbas, they had healing, restorative sleep after dreamwork with Paimon. How many of you feel like you haven't slept at all after a successful dreamwork session? How many of you felt completely relaxed? Does this change with the Daemon you're working with?

Week 7 - Amon - Invocation/Evocation #1

For those of you who wrote the letter to Amon, perform your evocation, then draw Amon's energy through you, and channel him to write his letter back to you.

For those of you who didn't - spend some time working divination with the Daemon.

Week 7 - Amon - Invocation/Evocation #2

Today, you can either choose to burn a request to Amon (sealed with a single drop of your blood, or a kiss) or you can do a divination session (traditional scrying or other).

Week 7 - Amon - Create a Spell or Ritual

Today, try creating a spell or ritual for reconciliation with an old friend, family member, co-worker. You don't necessarily have to perform it. Just create it and leave it in your journal for another day.

Week 7 - Amon - Reflect/Plan/Meditate/Rest

Use today to plan your upcoming week, and to either rest or meditate as you need to.

Are there any final reflections you'd like to share in your journal about your weeklong work with Amon?

WEEK 8: BARBATOS

DUKE
Color: Green
Incense: Sandalwood
Metal: Copper
Planet: Venus
Element: Fire
Enn: Eveta fubin Barbatos
Date: June 1-10

Original Purpose: Can give the ability to understand animals. Finds things hidden by magicians. Knows all things (divination) and conciliates friends and people in power.

Author's Notes: Seek Barbatos to stop magicians' personal wars with one another. Invoke Barbatos to communicate with your familiar if needed. Also invoke Barbatos to protect your home from hidden attacks.

Week 8 - Barbatos - Meditation

This week I want you to try a meditation where you spend some time not only focusing on Barbatos' seal, but also projecting your inner light outward, obliterating all negativity from you, your space and your home.

How do you feel after this meditation? Empowered? Drained?

Week 8 - Barbatos - Freewrite

Today I would like you to do a freewrite about Barbatos and the power of voice. Barbatos presides over sounds and language (the vocalization) of all creatures. What wisdom can he give you about your own voice (and I don't mean this superficially). Are you being heard? Do you speak up for yourself? Are you communicating your needs and boundaries to others?

If you choose not to do this you can either fill in your workbook spaces by preparing a ritual, or contemplating where Barbatos might fall on your Tree of Life/Death.

Week 8- Barbatos - Dreamwork

Tonight, when you go into your dreamwork, I want you to go in with the intention of protecting your mental and dream space. Visualize a protection ritual and call on Barbatos as you're falling asleep.

What does this dream produce? Do you feel calmer when you wake up? As the weeks go on, is the Dreamwork easier? Harder? Hit or miss?

Week 8 - Barbatos - Invocation/Evocation #1

Today I want you to focus on vocalization and sound and changing the energy of the room. Then, once the energy in the room changes, I want you to perform a divination.

For more advanced students - Perform a full Goetic Ritual, but focus on the quality and vibration of sound before seeking the Daemon in the Triangle of Art.

Week 8: Barbatos - Invocation/Evocation #2

Today I'd like you to Invoke Barbatos and ask him to help you in an area he excels in whether it be reconciling friendships, finding hidden information, or checking to see if a spell has been placed on you. If you need help from a pendulum or scrying device, go ahead and try that.

More Advanced Students: Use this time to ward your astral temple with the help of Barbatos.

Week 8: Barbatos - Create Spell/Ritual

Today, create one of two spells/rituals. Either write up a spell or ritual to stop a conflict utilizing Barbatos or create a ritual to ward your home with the influence of Barbatos.

Week 8: Barbatos – Rest / Reflect / Plan / Meditate

How did this week go for you? Did you resonate with Barbatos? How did you find his energy?

WEEK 9: PAIMON

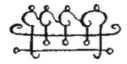

KING
Color: Yellow
Incense: Frankincense
Metal: Gold
Planet: Sun
Element: Water
Enn: Linan tasa jedan Paimon
Date: June 11 - 20

Original Purpose: He teaches all arts and sciences and occult. He can be invoked to bind others. To be observed toward the west and with offerings.

Author's Notes: Seek Paimon to understand alchemy. Seek Paimon for creative pursuits or to design a plan of action. Paimon can also help in emotional understanding.

Week 9 - Paimon – Meditate

Meditate on Paimon's sigil today. Feel him out. What kind of things can he help you with? What's going on in your life that may have an emotional slant? Remember that Water Daemons often take an emotional angle to things, and working with them effectively can sometimes require us to look at our feelings and why we do the things we do or react the way we react to a situation.

Week 9 – Paimon - Freewrite

This exercise can be extremely cathartic. It's essentially - giving the Daemonic divine your emotional burden. Not because it will be gone once you do it, but because you've been able to get it out and share it (with the Daemonic, but still). The Daemonic won't judge, and Paimon may even give you some help to ease your burdens.

Today, I want you to get all your frustrations and emotions out onto the page. Write about everything pissing you off, making you sad or angry, and about feelings you may not be comfortable sharing with anyone but the Daemonic. Get it all out.

Then - I want you to draw Paimon's seal across every page you've written, rip the pages from your notebook - and burn them while asking Paimon to ease your emotional burden. How do you feel after this exercise?

Week 9 - Paimon - Dreamwork

Go ahead and do your usual dreamwork and record any dreams.

Week 9 - Paimon - Invocation/Evocation #1

Today I want you to invoke Paimon for one of the following reasons:

1. After invoking him into your space - create something from deep in your emotional core. This could be music, art, writing, or even just jotting notes for an idea.

2. After invoking him into your space - confront a deep emotional trauma. Let it all out. If you have to cry, scream, or beat on a pillow or punching bag -- do it. Seriously.

3. After invoking him, ask for emotional peace.

4. Ask him to stop gossip or other people's attacks on you.

You can also do your own thing.

Week 9 - Paimon - Invocation/Evocation #2

Yes - this is a repeat. Choose something different from the list today:

1. After invoking him into your space - create something from deep in your emotional core. This could be music, art, writing, or even just jotting notes for an idea.

2. After invoking him into your space - confront a deep emotional trauma. Let it all out. If you have to cry, scream, or beat on a pillow or punching bag -- do it. Seriously.

3. After invoking him, ask for emotional peace.

4. Ask him to stop gossip or other people's attacks on you.

You can also do your own thing.

Week 9 - Paimon - Create a Spell or Ritual

So many rituals/spells - so little time.

Create a spell or ritual to draw Paimon into your life to inspire the emotional side of your creativity.

Or - alternatively:

Create a spell or ritual including Paimon to stop gossip and/or haters right in their tracks.

Week 9 - Paimon - Rest/Reflect/Plan/Meditate

How was your week working with Paimon? Do you feel you know him better? Did you gain valuable insight?

WEEK 10: BUER

PRESIDENT
Color: Orange
Incense: Storax
Metal: Mercury
Planet: Mercury
Element: Fire
Enn: Erato on ca Buer anon
Date: June 21 – July 1

Original Purpose: He teaches herbalism and herbal medicines. He heals emotional discord, gives good familiars, and also teaches philosophy and logic.

Author's Notes: Seek Buer to transform the self through thought, including rectifying addiction or bad behaviors. Invoke Buer for his wisdom about when magick is warranted and when it is not. He can help you weigh moral issues and help you distinguish between what is moral and what is natural. Morality is oftentimes something imposed on us by society, like taking a gift to a hostess for example. Whereas it might be a more natural inclination to show up empty handed unless you really wanted to bring her something. So basically, are you doing what you're doing because it's expected, or does it come from the heart and a genuine desire?

Week 10 - Buer - Meditate

Meditate on Buer and think of any bad habits you'd like to start transforming this week. Is it addiction? Overeating? Lack of exercise? Procrastination? What can you look at inwardly this week and begin transforming?

Alternatively - if the self-transformation is too weighty for you this week - this would be a good week to plan your herb garden and gain knowledge of herbalism from the Daemonic.

Week 10 - Buer - Freewrite

Today, I want you to look at the emotional reasons for the behaviors in yourself you want to change. Why are you overeating? Is there an emotional component? Why are you procrastinating on specific things? Are you bored? Scared? Anxious? Is there a way to make monotonous chores or projects more palatable? Think of solutions to these issues. Would eating more frequent, smaller meals help? Will using a smaller plate help with portion control? Is there a way to get more exercise into your daily routine without it seeming/feeling like

boring exercise?
Now calm your mind, invoke Buer, and look over
what you've written. What does he have to say on
the matter? Any advice? Write it down.

Alternatively - draw out your perfect herb garden,
or choose a place in your home where you can put
a few plants in the window. Growing your own
medicinal/culinary herbs can be very rewarding
and you can imbue the plants with their magickal
purpose at the time you plant the seeds. It may also
be time to grab a few pots and some seeds so you
can plant seeds during invocation.

Week 10 - Buer - Dreamwork

Tonight, I want you to go into your dreamwork
visualizing the perfect outcome to your self-
transformation. What does the dream tell you?
Alternatively - if you're doing the herb garden
project - visualize yourself standing in a beautiful
garden. What does this visualization do for your
dreaming self?

Week 10 - Buer - Invocation/Evocation #1

Today, invoke Buer and then:

1. If you're doing self-transformation -- Draw
   that Buer energy into your body and bask in
   his transformative energy.

2. If you're planting herbs (or even a single herb), invoke Buer over the pot with soil in it, plant the seeds, and visualize Buer's energy fortifying and strengthening the plant that will eventually grow.
3. Place the pot in a sunny window or under a grow lamp.

Remember, it's perfectly okay to simply reflect on Buer and bask in his energy this week.

Week 10 - Buer - Invocation/Evocation #2

Invoke Buer today into every room of your home with the intent to bring positive transformation to you, and everyone in your home.

If you are working with Buer for herbalism - Focus on your plant(s) again and give them that Buer Energy.

For more advanced students: Remember that it's also okay to do your standard Goetic scrying ritual to speak with the Daemon and gain wisdom and insight.

Week 10 - Buer - Create a Spell or Ritual

Today - create a spell or ritual for self-transformation.

OR

Create a spell or ritual to imbue your herb(s) with healing/transformational properties.

Week 10 - Buer - Plan/Rest/Reflect/Meditate

What was your favorite part of your work with Buer? I know that Rome wasn't built in a day, and lasting transformation takes time, but did you feel any transformation? If you did the herb project - how did planting a pot make you feel? Did you gain any interesting insight into what you should plant or why?

WEEK 11: GUSION

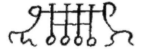

DUKE
Color: Green
Incense: Sandalwood
Metal: Copper
Planet: Venus
Element: Water
Enn: Secore vesa anet Gusion
Date: July 2 -11

Original Purpose: He knows all past, present and things to come. He can answer questions and tell you why you ask them. He conciliates and reconciles friendships and gives honor and dignity to those who seek it.

Author's Notes: If you are looking to find your faults or to do deep self-work, Gusion is the Daemon to work with. He holds a mirror up to your face and causes you to see your true self.

Week 11 - Gusion - Meditation

Today, I want you to meditate on the sigil, then slowly turn your focus into yourself. Are you being your truest, most authentic self? If not? What is holding you back? Bringing Gusion's energy into the space then looking at yourself can be a rather revealing experience. For those more advanced, try drawing the Daemon's sigil on a mirror (black or silver depending on your skill level or what you have on hand) and looking into it. Be sure to use a substance for the sigil that will wipe clean, like a Daemonic or scrying oil, or just plain olive oil.

Week 11 - Gusion - Freewrite

Today in your journal, I dare you to list three of your flaws. Next, draw Gusion's seal on the page and focus on him. Now, reach into the divine intelligence (from within yourself) and brainstorm why these are flaws and what you can do to correct them.

Yes, the deeper down the rabbit hole we go, the deeper the path work gets.

Week 11 - Gusion - Dreamwork

Do your dreamwork as usual, but today, try going in with the goal to see what your authentic self actually looks like. How does (s)he sound? How does (s)he carry themselves? What is different?

Week 11 - Gusion - Invocation/Evocation #1

Today we're going to confront our faults. Invoke/Evoke Gusion and ask him to show you what's wrong. This can be a jarring exercise for some people, so go into it knowing that you may be faced with something that isn't pretty. This exercise has even scared a few folks in the past. Now, the second you feel an emotional response to what you're seeing, I want you to attack it. You can do this in your head, or you can verbally attack it (if you're not going to cause discord in your home by doing so).

Alternatives would be draw Gusion's strength into you to bring out your authentic self.

For more ceremonial magicians, remember - you're welcome to do the Goetic work by the book.
And for those of you who find yourself too busy, try a MOVING meditation after invoking Gusion. Gentle yoga or a long walk may be in order.

Week 11 - Gusion - Invocation/Evocation #2

Look at yesterday's suggestions for exercises and choose a different one today.

Week 11 – Gusion - Create a Spell or Ritual

Today, create a spell or ritual to see your true self,

or to invoke/evoke your authentic self.

Week 11 - Gusion - Rest/Reflect/Meditate/Plan

What did the past week teach you about yourself?

For those of you still with us -- great job! You're doing fantastic and I'm so proud of all of you sticking it out through 11 weeks. About this time we lose a few folks who just didn't have the time they wanted to devote to this immersion. So, if you're still here - even if you're just spending a few minutes in meditation every day - I applaud your perseverance and dedication.

I hope you're all getting a lot out of this immersion experience. It's a hard one!

WEEK 12: SITRI

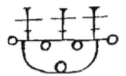

PRINCE
Color: Blue
Incense: Cedar
Metal: Tin
Planet: Jupiter
Element: Earth
Enn (also Sytry): Lirach Alora vefa Sitri
Date: July 12 - 21

Original Purpose: Sitri is a lust demon and causes men and women to be passionate and get naked around one another.

Author's Notes: Invoke Sitri for seduction rituals (become Incubi or Succubi). Invoke Sitri during sex magick to boost the energy raised. Sitri can also be called up when you seek to infuse any creative project with passion. I saw Sitri as feminine and Fire.

Week 12- Sitri – Meditation

Today I want you to draw Sitri's sigil while thinking of all the things you're passionate about. Now gaze at the sigil (gentle eyelids, relaxed facial muscles) and remember what you see, feel, hear, and experience during this exercise.

Week 12 - Sitri - Freewrite

Today, I want you to explore your passions or your sexuality in your journal. Write about your hopes and dreams. Of lovers or of love lost. Just 10 minutes. If you're struggling, start with "I love..." or "I am passionate about..." If it turns into an erotic story, great. If it turns into a memoir of your first lover, great. If it turns into a diary of all your hopes and dreams, that's fantastic, too!

Week 12 - Sitri - Dreamwork

Tonight, as you're concentrating on Sitri and focusing all she stands for. You can go into this dream looking for a sexual encounter, or you can go in visualizing whatever you're passionate about. Hopefully you'll get some advice or inspiration or have an encounter that brings you much needed release.

Week 12 - Sitri - Invocation/Evocation #1

Choose from one of the following:

1. Speak with Sitri in the scrying mirror.
2. Draw the energy of Sitri into you for heightened sexuality or sexual confidence.
3. Request that Sitri give you inspiration.

Week 12 - Sitri - Invocation/Evocation #2

Choose a different one. (It's like choose your own adventure)

1. Speak with Sitri in the scrying mirror.
2. Draw the energy of Sitri into you for heightened sexuality or sexual confidence.
3. Request that Sitri give you inspiration.

Week 12 - Sitri - Create a Spell or Ritual

Create a spell or ritual to bring out your sexuality, or to find inspiration for your passions, or to find your passion.

Week 12 - Sitri - Rest/Plan/Meditate/Reflect

What did this week teach you about the Daemon and yourself?

Only 64 more weeks to go! You can do this!

WEEK 13: BELETH

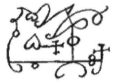

KING
Color: Yellow
Incense: Frankincense
Metal: Gold
Planet: Sun
Element: Earth
Enn: Lirach tasa vefa wehlc Beleth
Date: July 22 – August 1

Original Purpose: Beleth is described as terrifying and it is said the magician must keep a hazel wand at the ready to keep Beleth's fury and flaming breath at bay. Causes love and desire.

Author's Notes: While Beleth can be invoked as a lust Daemon, his purpose is better suited to actual work where you are seeking a soul mate or long-term companion or stable relationship. He can also give counsel in matters of the heart and help bring rational thinking to highly emotional matters regarding loved ones. Seek Beleth after death of a loved one to find stability and comfort.

Week 13 - Beleth - Meditation

Today I want you to merely spend time with the sigil and draw it a few times while considering Beleth's role as both one who soothes grief and helps in mourning of a loss (not just of loved ones, but loss of a job, loss of physical capability, loss of dependence or independence etc...) and one who brings rational thinking to emotional matters. Now look at your own life and ask yourself what you've lost, or what emotional/passionate areas of your life could use some down-to-Earth pragmatism.

Week 13 – Beleth- Freewrite

Today, write about one of the following:

1. Something/Someone you're currently grieving.
2. An emotional situation that you could use some perspective on.
3. What do you desire? Could pertain to a relationship, or something you're passionate about.

Week 13 - Beleth - Dreamwork

Tonight, do your before-bed dreamwork prep as usual and as you're falling asleep, think of Beleth or focus on his seal. Then let whatever happens, happens. Record any dreams first thing when you wake up.

Week 13 - Beleth - Invocation/Evocation #1

Invoke Beleth and sit with him for a short time, feeling out his energy and how it feels against your own. Ask him to be present and reveal any wisdom you should know. Record any thoughts (especially if they feel like they're coming from your higher self or outside the self). Record sensations, feelings, smells, or sounds.

More Advanced: Invoke Beleth, go into ascension, and ask for a personal invocation (enn) to draw him to you more readily. If you need more information about ascension practice - read *Lake of Fire: A Daemonolater's Guide to Ascension* by S. Connolly.

Week 13 - Beleth - Invocation/Evocation #2

Today I want you to invoke Beleth, write on a sheet of paper what you want/need within his scope of influence, then place a drop of blood on the paper (optional), then burn it. Thank Beleth and close the ritual.

How did you feel after this experience?

Week 13 - Beleth - Create a Spell or Ritual

Today I want you to create one of the following:

1. A spell/ritual for grieving that draws on Beleth's influence.
2. A spell/ritual for clear sight into an emotional situation.

As usual, if you are simply spending a week to meditate on each Daemon, this is fine, too.

Week 13 - Beleth - Rest/Reflect/Meditate/Plan

How did work with Beleth help you this week? How did you find his energy? How did it combine with yours? Do keep track of how burning the request manifests in days and weeks to come.

WEEK 14: LERAJE

MARQUIS
Color: Violet
Incense: Jasmine
Metal: Silver
Planet: Moon
Element: Fire
Enn: (also Leraikha)- Caymen vefa Leraje
Date: August 2 - 11

Original Purpose: He causes battles and strife and can cause wounds to putrefy.

Author's Notes: Aside from general execration magick, you can seek the wisdom of Leraje during conflicts in order to resolve them. Leraje also gives good counsel to those seeking help in relationships with difficult people.

Week 14 - Leraje - Meditation

Meditate on the sigil for a few minutes, then turn your focus inward starting with observing your breath. As you start to examine your current state, it's likely that any conflicts (even internal) going on in your life are bound to float to the surface. As you're thinking of these challenges, impose a visualization of Leraje's sigil on top of these obstacles. Now return your focus to your breath, close your eyes, and listen.

What happens? Record your experience in your journal.

Week 14 - Leraje - Freewrite

Today, I'd like you to write about any self-limiting beliefs, problems, or situations that have been an obstacle to any area of your life. What solutions have you tried? What haven't you tried? Why? Find the main thing bothering you and expand on that. What can you do to change your situation?
This may also be a good opportunity to try the "letter writing" exercise again, where you write to the Daemon about your problem and ask for advice.

Also consider that Leraje can help things move forward at a brisker pace. Perhaps things are taking too long. Or you're stuck procrastinating? It's amazing how many problems we have in life can be fixed by examining ourselves, both in emotion and action, to find the solution.

Week 14 - Leraje - Dreamwork

Tonight, go into sleep with an open mind. Focus on

the sigil as you drift to sleep (or even the enn), and let whatever happens, happen. See if you get a message, or come out of sleep with more energy, solutions to problems, or even some inspiration.

Week 14 - Leraje - Invocation/Evocation #1

Choose one of the following exercises:

1. Ascension practice, in which case you can obtain your own enn and/or variant sigil to work with Leraje.
2. Invoke/Evoke Leraje and draw his energy into you in order to have more energy to get things done.
3. Invoke/Evoke the Daemon and simply burn a request in his presence, then thank him and close the ritual.

Week 14 - Leraje - Invocation/Evocation #2

Choose a different one today:

1. Ascension practice, in which case you can obtain your own enn and/or variant sigil to work with Leraje.
2. Invoke/Evoke Leraje and draw his energy into you in order to have more energy to get things done.
3. Invoke/Evoke the Daemon and simply burn a request in his presence, then thank him and

close the ritual.

You're always welcome to do your own work as well.

Week 14 - Leraje - Create a Spell or Ritual

Today, create a spell or ritual for one of the following:

1. To start or finish any altercation.
2. To get the ball rolling on a project.
3. To remove emotional blockages.

Week 14 - Leraje - Rest/Reflect/Meditate/Plan

What insights did working with Leraje provide? How did your energy mesh with his/hers/theirs?

WEEK 15: ELIGOS

DUKE
Color: Green
Incense: Sandalwood
Metal: Copper
Planet: Venus
Element: Water
Enn: (Also Eligios) Jedan on ca Eligos inan
Date: August 12 - 22

Original Purpose: Discover hidden things, knows things to come, and knows about war and how soldiers will come to meet.

Author's Notes: This Daemon is another good one to consult when seeking advice during a feud. He also gives good counsel on when to use magick and can tell you if someone is causing you harm via magick.

Week 15 - Eligos - Meditate

This week, while meditating on Eligos' seal, I want you to visualize your third eye opening. Imagine the sigil where your third eye should be. Draw a picture if it helps. You may also anoint the third eye with some tiger balm to bring awareness to that part of your body.

Week 15 – Eligos - Freewrite

Today I want you to write down at least five questions you'd like the answer to. You should have at least one of the answers by the end of the week. Make sure they are one-part questions. Oftentimes, when people ask questions, they try to shove 6 questions into one. Example: Will I get the new job and if so will I like it and will I like the people I'm working with. That's 3 questions folks. Not one. So list your questions as you'll be trying to get answers to them this week. (The list can be edited or pondered on.)

Week 15 - Eligos – Dreamwork

Tonight, I want you to take one of your questions and focus on it (along with the Daemon's seal) before bed. Try to fall asleep while seeking the answer. Make sure you're keeping your dream journal and a working pen handy so you can immediately jot down any dreams you remember immediately upon waking.

Did you get an answer?

Week 15 - Eligos - Invocation/Evocation #1

Today I want you to invoke/evoke Eligos and perform a divination session. You can use whatever divination device you choose. Use a pendulum with a few baseline questions if you're not clairvoyant or clairaudient. Remember that using the divination device dependent on your existing gifts will make for stronger results. For more information about this, see Drawing Down Belial.

Ask for answers to some or all of your written questions. See what the answers are and write them down.

Close the ritual by thanking the Daemon for being present.

Week 15 - Eligos - Invocation/Evocation #2

Today I want you to invoke/evoke Eligos and write up a request, asking him to bring you answers. You may add a drop of blood to this, then burn it in the offering bowl. Feel free to spend some time in reflection before closing the ritual.

OR

You can repeat the divination session with the same, or different, questions.
MORE ADVANCED: Do your invocation then go into ascension and speak with the Daemon directly

about your questions.

Be sure to note all the information you receive once you close the ritual.

For the Ceremonialists among you - a traditional Goetic evocation (with your modifications as needed) is also a good choice for this second session.

Week 15 - Eligos - Create and Spell or Ritual

Try one of the following:

1. Write a spell/ritual for clear sight utilizing the energy of Eligos.

2. Enchant one of your divination devices with the energy of Eligos and keep it for future divination sessions. It can be a mirror, a pendulum, or even the creation of a seal you can use on your altar during divination sessions.

Week 15 – Eligos - Rest/Meditate/Reflect/Plan

Use this day to reflect on your week and plan for the upcoming week of workings.

Remember that even if all you're doing is carrying the Daemon's seal, or giving them 5 minutes of reflection each night, that's okay.

Any observations to write in your notebook? Feel

free to write your own questions and answers in reflection of your week.

WEEK 16: ZEPAR

DUKE
Color: Green
Incense: Sandalwood
Metal: Copper
Planet: Venus
Element: Earth
Enn: Lyan Ramec catya Zepar
Date: August 23 – September 1

Original Purpose: He causes women to love men and also makes women barren.

Author's Notes: Likewise, Zepar can be invoked as a fertility Daemon. Invoke Zepar to find your marriage partner.

Week 16 - Zepar - Meditate

For you meditation today, start by drawing the sigil and focusing on Zepar, then slowly shift your focus to your relationships. Not just romantic relationships. Remember, there are many types of love. There's platonic love, there's romantic love, there's self-love. As usual, expect that the thing you may need to work on in your relationships (even if that relationship is with yourself) will float to the top. Your job today isn't to try to solve your relationship issues, or sit and wallow in self-pity, or stew over your best friend's comment about something. It's to observe any thoughts that come up and your emotional reactions to them as if you were standing outside yourself looking in. What did this exercise show you? Jot some notes in your journal.

Week 16 - Zepar - Freewrite

Today, I want you to draw the seal of Zepar in your journal and then start by writing down things you'd like to change, encourage, or stop doing in your relationships and why.

Week 16 - Zepar - Dreamwork

For those of you in happy relationships, simply focus on the sigil, slip it under your pillow or mattress, and sleep on it. See if anything comes up.

For those of you seeking happier relationships, especially romantic ones, try focusing on Zepar, then shifting your focus to your they type of person you'd like to have in your life as you fall asleep. See what comes up.

Regardless which exercise you choose, be sure to

write anything you remember in your dream journal.

Week 16 - Zepar - Invocation/Evocation #1

For those in happy relationships: Invoke Zepar and ask him to bless your relationship(s) with strength and longevity.

For those seeking happier relationships: Invoke Zepar and ask him to bring the right person/people to you.

Week 16 - Zepar - Invocation/Evocation #2

Draw Zepar into your temple and bask in any feelings of love that come up. Draw that love into yourself and vow to share that love with others today.

OR - Invoke the Daemon during ascension and speak with him about the nature of your relationships.

OR - Invoke the Daemon into a visage of the partner you wish to have and ask the Daemon to bring them to you.

You can also invoke the Daemon to help with fertility and having children.

Week 16 - Zepar - Create a Spell or Ritual

Create a spell or ritual with Zepar to draw stronger, healthier relationships into your life.

OR

Create a spell or ritual with Zepar to draw self-love.

Week 16 - Zepar - Plan/Rest/Reflect/Meditate

Did this week working with Zepar give you any insight into your relationships that hadn't occurred to you before? Did you try working with him for self-love? If so, would you do it again? Be sure to take notes on all the noteworthy realizations you had this past week.

WEEK 17: BOTIS

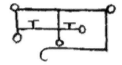

PRESIDENT
Color: Orange
Incense: Storax
Metal: Mercury
Planet: Mercury
Element: Water
Enn: Jedan hoesta noc ra Botis
Date: September 2 - 11

Original Purpose: He tells things past and to come and can reconcile friends and foes.

Author's Notes: Most Water Daemons can be invoked for emotional matters with regard to relationships. Seek Botis to draw new friends or perform divination regarding friends.

Week 17 - Botis - Meditation

Today, I want you to draw or paint Botis's sigil. Find a "Daemonic Arts & Crafts" way of creating the sigil. While you're creating, I want you to focus on Botis' purpose, or his enn. How do you feel after this meditation?

Week 17 - Botis - Freewrite

What can you learn from Botis? Do you need advice in friendships/relationships? Divination to discover what's going on? Closure from a friendship/relationship that hurt you? Write about all of this in your journal and see what wisdom you gain from it.

Week 17 - Botis - Dreamwork

Tonight, as you're falling asleep with the sigil under the pillow/mattress, or within view, concentrate on setting your intent to speak with the Daemon in the dream. You can also speak the enn or ascend into the astral temple. Whichever is easiest for you.

You can also go into sleep with the intent of seeing the future or finding answers or solving a particular problem. Be creative here. Don't be afraid to experiment. You may find something that works better for you.

Note: Some folks anoint themselves with the scent of the Daemon they're working with. In this case, anointing with a tincture of benzoin (as most witches have this) should be fine. Be sure to test all oils/tinctures on the back of your hand before anointing the third eye or wrists.

Week 17 - Botis - Evocation/Invocation #1

So many friendship/relationship Daemons, so little time. Choose one of the following and give it a go.

1. Invoke the Daemon and present him with a problem and the resolution you'd like to see. Burn this as a request. Thank the Daemonic for being present. Close the ritual standard.

2. Do a divination session with the Daemon.

3. Invoke the Daemon, head into Ascension, and work with the Daemon on anything you choose. Self-work on emotional trauma's involving other people might be a good choice here.
Tomorrow - you'll pick a different one.

Week 17 - Botis - Evocation/Invocation #2

Choose one of the following and give it a go.

1. Invoke the Daemon and present him with a problem and the resolution you'd like to see. Burn this as a request. Thank the Daemonic for being present. Close the ritual standard.

2. Do a divination session with the Daemon.
3. Invoke the Daemon, head into Ascension, and work with the Daemon on anything you choose. Self-work on emotional trauma's involving other

people might be a good choice here.

You are also welcome to do your own thing. Remember that the daily assignments are only suggestions and are meant to inspire you to your own Great Work.

Week 17 - Botis - Create a Spell or Ritual

Today, create a spell or ritual in which you draw the energy of Botis to:

1. Bring clarity to a relationship.
2. Reconcile relationships.
3. For Divination

Or whatever else you might come up with. Be sure to write it in your journal (leave space for notes or future results) so you don't forget it.

Week 17 - Botis - Plan/Reflect/Rest/Meditate

Spend a few minutes reflecting on the past week. If you're journaling, go ahead and write down your observations or general feelings about Botis.

WEEK 18: BATHIN

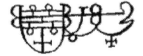

DUKE
Color: Green
Incense: Sandalwood
Metal: Copper
Planet: Venus
Element: Earth
Enn: Dyen Pretore on ca Bathin
Date: September 12 - 22

Original Purpose: Knows the virtues of herbs and precious stones and can transport people from one country to another.

Author's Notes: Invoke Bathin before travel for a smooth trip. Also keep his sigil on you. You can invoke Bathin to bring you opportunity for travel as well. Kitchen witchery will get you further with Bathin than ceremony.

Week 18 - Bathin - Meditation

Today, weather permitting of course, I want you to take a pen and paper outside and draw the seal while in nature. Breath deep and purposefully while you draw and consider the Daemonic. Spend 10 minutes breathing in the fresh air.

Backyards and parks are perfect for this exercise. If the only place you can do the exercise is outside during your lunch hour, do it then. Since Bathin rules over natural magick, a natural setting and getting back to nature seems appropriate. Consider that for your forthcoming work this week.

Week 18 - Bathin - Freewrite

Again, go outside to do this exercise if you can. Otherwise, sit near a window where you can see outside and be inspired by nature. When you think of Bathin, what does he remind you of? Where would you like to travel? What do you often imagine? How do the natural elements of magick make you feel? Write about whatever comes to mind. These are just some suggested prompts. You can make up your own.

Week 18 - Bathin - Dreamwork

Tonight, I want you to visualize a serene outdoor dreamscape as you fall asleep. Visualize yourself leaving your body and moving into this natural setting and sit quietly. Are you able to lift out of your body? This can take some practice. If you can take control of the situation and explore the natural dreamscape, try to find Bathin and converse with him.

What were your results with this dreamwork? Write this down in your journal.

Week 18 - Bathin - Evocation/Invocation #1

Today, I want you to invoke/evoke Bathin into your ritual space. Now, on a sheet of paper, I want you to write down any places you'd like to go in your lifetime. Your plans can be grand and lofty like "Travel the World!" and/or more realistic like "A romantic weekend getaway with my partner." Sign the piece of paper with your name. Draw Bathin's sigil on it. Hold it between your palms for a few moments, imagining yourself at your destination. Then utter the words: "Manifesting! So be it." Now burn this in the offering bowl while visualizing your request rising to meet Bathin. Let's see what comes of you putting this intention out into the world. Write down the operation in your journal. The point of the journal is to review it every few years. See what's happened. What's manifested. You may want to leave space for future notes.

Week 18 - Bathin - Evocation/Invocation #2

You are welcome to do your own thing, but here are some suggestions for today's experiment:

1. Draw the Daemon into the scrying mirror for a

chat. It could be about natural magick, or increasing your visualization skills. It can also be in relation to matters of travel, or to help you learn a skill like astral travel.

2. Bring some art supplies into the ritual space, draw the Daemon into the space, and then create whatever you're inspired to create.

3. Bring several stones and herbs into the ritual space. Draw the Daemon into the space, then hold each item and see what impression you get from it. If you hold a black tourmaline, how does it feel? What is your instinct to use it for? Let the Daemonic energy guide you and listen to your intuition. Record all of this in your journal.

Week 18 - Bathin - Create a Spell or Ritual

See if you can create a spell or ritual from one of the following (or come up with your own thing):
1. A spell to learn natural magick.
2. A spell to bring opportunities for travel.
3. A spell or ritual for astral travel.
4. A meditation ritual with Bathin utilizing natural stones and visualization.

Week 18 - Bathin - Rest/Reflect/Meditate/Plan

What did you learn from your work with Bathin this

week? Did he impart any knowledge of natural magick? How did you find his energy? Did you vibe with it?

WEEK 19: SALLOS

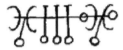

DUKE
Color: Green
Incense: Sandalwood
Metal: Copper
Planet: Venus
Element: Earth
Enn: (also Saleos) - Serena Alora Sallos Aken
Date: September 23 – October 2

Original Purpose: Sallos is invoked to cause men to love women and women to love men.

Author's Notes: Comparable to Rosier in the Dukanté Hierarchy. Sallos can be invoked during marriage ceremonies.

Week 19 - Sallos - Meditation

This week, as you're drawing the sigil, I want you to draw it with confidence. Find that confident part of you and bask in your own greatness. Now, before you start lecturing me on the detriment of ego, remember that this is just an exercise. What other parts of your life could use a confidence boost right now? Who could you work to influence to your way of thinking? Remember that Sallos rules over confidence, glamour magick, as well as love and lust magick.

Week 19 - Sallos - Freewrite

Thinking of Sallos, just write. See what comes of it. The whole purpose of freewriting is to get things out of your head and on paper. Sometimes it brings revelation. Other times it brings clarity and understanding. There is no right or wrong way to do this exercise.

If you need a writing prompt: What areas of your life are you lacking confidence? Why is that? What can you do to change it? (If you want to change it, of course.)

Week 19 - Sallos - Dreamwork

As usual, place the seal beneath the pillow or mattress. (Or on a white board above the bed, or whatever works for you.) You can try one of the following.

1. Go into the dream realm determined to meet your soul mate.

2. Go into the dream being who you want to be. Becoming that person.

Tomorrow - write your results up in your dream journal.

Week 19 - Sallos - Invocation/Evocation #1

Today - I want you to draw Sallos into your ritual space and summon your own confidence (that Sallos part of you!) at the same time.

After the experiment consider the following questions in your journal:

1. How did the experiment turn out?

2. Can I find a shortened way to evoke this feeling from within myself at will? (Think of this for this week's create a spell/ritual exercise).

3. How does Sallos's energy make me feel?

Week 19 - Sallos - Invocation/Evocation #2

Today, invoke/evoke the Daemon into a scrying mirror or ball (i.e. triangle of art for those of you who have constructed a proper one). Ask any question that you find relevant.

Advanced: Consider working ascension to meet with the Daemonic force directly for any questions you may have, or problems you need solutions or answers for.

Week 19 - Sallos - Create a Spell or Ritual

This week - create a spell or ritual with Sallos for Glamour, Love, or Confidence.

Week 19 - Sallos - Rest/Reflect/Meditate/Plan

How did working with Sallos affect how you see yourself? Think of how you carry yourself. How you communicate. How you interact with others (especially body language and cadence of speech.) Reflect on this. What lessons from the week will you carry forward with you?

WEEK 20: PURSON

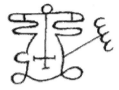

KING
Color: Yellow
Incense: Frankincense
Metal: Gold
Planet: Sun
Element: Earth
Enn: Ana secore on ca Purson
Date: October 3 - 12

Original Purpose: Uncover hidden things, divination, and discover treasure. Answers truthfully all questions both earthly and divine. He brings good familiars.

Author's Notes: Purson is a great Daemon to work with during scrying or channeling sessions when you have questions about the Divine Intelligences (i.e. Daemons) or are seeking to better understand their nature. Also, a Daemon to consult before any scientific experimentation so that answers can be found. A Daemon of natural sciences.

Week 20 - Purson - Meditation

This week, you might try picking a single theme. Are you looking to explore the Daemonic Divine? Are you wanting to work on your divination skills? Or are you looking for your Great Work or life's calling (if you haven't already found it)?

As you're drawing and meditating on his seal today, consider what the Daemon can help you with right now. I definitely recommend some ascension work with Purson for those of you comfortable with that.

Week 20 - Purson - Freewrite

Today's prompt - what is your relationship with the natural world around you? Think about all the ways you fit into the vast universe. Think about your heart's urge. What are your strengths? If you had a calling, what would you say it is? You can be specific or general. What themes (things you are often called on for) resurface in your life frequently? Where are you often asked to help?

Bonus assignment: Ask one friend and one family member the following question: If there was a calling I missed, what would you say it was?

Don't be surprised if the answer is something unexpected. My sister-in-law of 33 years thinks I should have worked with children, which makes me chuckle every time she says it. What she's actually seeing is my natural affinity for teaching and inspiring others, including children, which is a huge part of my Great Work. Getting the answers to that question from others is merely for perspective.

Week 20 - Purson - Dreamwork

Tonight, during your dreamwork, I want you to concentrate on finding both spiritual and mundane answers to questions as they relate to your Great Work. Your ultimate purpose in life. You can think specifically, like you can say you want to be a great [insert specific profession or qualities here]. But think more generally. On a grander scale.

Week 20 - Purson - Invocation/Evocation #1

Today I want you to invoke/evoke Purson and scry with the Daemon. See what wisdom they have to offer you.

Advanced: Use a full Goetic ritual (modified, of course) to do the assignment.

Week 20 – Purson - Invocation/Evocation #2

Today, simply invoke the Daemon, write out a request, seal it with a drop of blood, and burn it in the offering bowl. Close the ritual. Note any sensations, sounds, smells, thoughts, emotions. Leave some space in your journal to revisit this experiment and note any results that might come of it.

Week 20 - Purson - Create a Spell/Ritual

Consider creating a spell or ritual for one of the following:

1. Discovering your Great Work

2. Getting to Know the Daemonic

3. For Gaining Wisdom/Knowledge

4. Divination on Matters of the Spirit

Week 20 - Purson - Rest/Reflect/Plan/Meditate

What did your week with Purson teach you about yourself and your own Great Work? For those of you who worked with him for other reasons - what did this week remind you of, or bring your attention to? Note all of this in your journal.

WEEK 21: MARAX

PRESIDENT
Color: Orange
Incense: Storax
Metal: Mercury
Planet: Mercury
Element: Earth
Enn: (also Narax) - Kaymen Vefa Marax
Date: October 12 - 22

Original Purpose: Imparts knowledge of astronomy and liberal sciences. He can also give good familiars that know the virtues of herbs and stones.

Author's Notes: Marax can come off a bit strong, like the too serious professor who doesn't tolerate the lazy student. Be disciplined when seeking his wisdom, influence, or guidance. A good Daemon to invoke before exams or during study to retain more information. His keyword is discipline.

Week 21 - Marax - Meditate

For today's meditation, I want you to sit and focus on the sigil for ten minutes. Concentrate on the lines. The flow of the sigil. Stare at it until you can close your eyes and see it.

Note how quickly you're able to form a mental image of this seal in your mind's eye. If you have difficulty sitting in silence for long periods of time, or difficulty with focus, try doing yoga with the seal in front of you where you can occasionally gaze at it. Or take a walk and glance at the sigil every so often. Focus on your breath and relaxing into your moving meditation.

Remember that there are different ways to meditate other than sitting in a silent room. The point being that there are many roads to the same goal. You just have to find the road you're most comfortable with.

Week 21 - Marax - Freewrite

While there are many reasons to work with Marax, one of those areas can be discipline. By all means, choose to work with Marax in your garden, to get familiars, or to study and retain information and knowledge, but a very good reason to work with this Daemon would be to cultivate discipline. Much like Thoth, Marax is a bit of a hard-ass when it comes to teaching because he expects students to be disciplined and will throw the same lesson at you over and over again until you improve, or at least learn something.

Today in your journal I want you to write down all the things you could be more disciplined in doing. Whether it's a task you always put off like putting your receipts in a certain folder, a personal thing you'd like to change about yourself such as dealing with conflict better, or just being more consistent in your study and practice -- write about it. Why do you put things off or deny yourself the time to apply yourself? Be honest. No one will see this journal except you. (You can burn the journal at the end of this class if you wish.) So be completely honest. How does the lack of discipline in this area make you feel? Do you think this is something Marax can help with. Do you even want to change?

Maybe you're not disciplined in this area because you really couldn't care less - and that's okay! You only have so much energy and time to apply to each day - and we make time for the things that are important to us. If it's not important, give yourself permission to let it go.

Write: "I [your name] give myself permission to NOT force myself to do [insert thing here] and I will be okay with that. This is not important to me at this time."
Maybe at some other time it will be important, but

chances are that time is not now.

But if it turns out something is important to you, it's important to express all of the reasons you are putting it off in order to get to the root cause. You may even find some insecurities or fears are the ultimate cause, in which case you know what you need to work on as this class progresses. Getting your anxieties, worries, and fears out onto the page can help you better create a plan of action to take these things on and work through them.

Week 21 - Marax - Dreamwork

Go into your dreamwork as usual. You probably have a system down by now. Whether it's gazing at the sigil, reciting the enn, or practicing some deep breathing or moving meditation before bed to get you in the right frame of mind - do what is working for you, or feel free to try a different method.

Tonight, if you run into the Daemon in the dream world, discuss with him the ways in which his wisdom may be able to help you this week. Try to take this out of the dream realm into the waking world and write it in your dream journal. Also note any symbolism.

Week 21 - Marax - Invocation/Evocation #1

During today's ritual to invoke/evoke Marax, I want you to do one of the following:

1. Burn a request asking the Daemon for his assistance in one of the areas he can help you.

2. Speak with them in the mirror or crystal (if you want to do a traditional scrying).

3. Just draw the Daemonic energy into the ritual space to sit with it for a while.

Week 21 - Marax - Invocation/Evocation #2

Today you can either pick a different item from yesterday's list or try drawing the essence of the Daemon into you as you set your mind to be more disciplined in a specific area of your life. Regardless of what you choose, make notes in your notebooks/workbooks and keep track of how these rituals and work with the Daemon manifests for you.

Now I also understand that you're not going to vibe with every Daemon you work with and if that's the case with Marax, that's okay, too. You might have better luck working with the same thing you wish to work on with another one of the Goetic spirits as the course progresses. So keep that in mind and if you and a Daemon don't seem to mesh, don't beat yourself up and think you've failed. You haven't. It's just not the right Daemonic force for you. You will only know which Daemons you work well with by working with them. Remember that.

Week 21 – Marax - Create a Spell or Ritual

Create a spell or ritual for one of the following:

1. Find a familiar.
2. Gain knowledge or deep study. (Focus)
3. To learn the virtues of stones and herbs.
4. To make your garden flourish.
5. A ritual/spell for discipline and/or developing routines.

Week 21 - Marax - Plan/Reflect/Rest/Meditate

What did this week teach you about yourself in areas of discipline? If you worked with the Daemon for another reason, what came of it? Did you get that familiar? Did you ask Marax to help your herb garden grow? Did you feel inspired to work more natural magick or buy some new stones? Perhaps you learned something new?

For those who are just using this time to reflect on each Daemon for a week - what insights did you have? Write this all in your journal for later perusal.

WEEK 22: IPOS

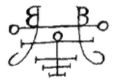

PRINCE
Color: Blue
Incense: Cedar
Metal: Tin
Planet: Jupiter
Element: Water
Enn: Desa an Ipos Ayer
Date: October 23 – November 1

Original Purpose: He knows all things and makes men witty and bold.

Author's Notes: Some texts say Ipos is an Earl and can use those correspondences (Mars/Iron/Red etc....) as well. Invoke Ipos for courage or to be more decisive. Ipos can also be invoked to sort out confusion or to bring your emotions under control.

Week 22 - Ipos - Meditate

Today, while meditating on Ipos and his seal, I want you seriously start looking at your confidence levels. and your emotional control. Additionally, if you're more experienced, you can visualize the sigil, then imagine that sigil taking up the space over your third eye, giving you additional insight, or opening the third eye even wider. Remember that divination/seeing can also apply to heightened intuition and empathy, or even changing your perspective to include new ideas and possibilities.

Week 22- Ipos - Freewrite

Today, explore issues of confidence, divination, decision making, intuition, perspective, and emotional control within yourself. Do you make decisions easily? What do you need perspective on? In what situations would you like to exert more emotional control? Do you trust your intuition? How confident are you in different areas of your life? You don't have to answer all of these questions in your journal. I simply provide the questions to inspire you to ask yourself some difficult questions and to explore the answers by writing it all out and getting it onto the page. When you're finished, you can close the journal and walk away, or you can read back over it and reflect on what you've read. How deep you go into these exercises is always up to you. But the deeper you go, often the greater the rewards in the long run. Do keep that in mind.

Week 22 - Ipos - Dreamwork

Tonight, go into your dreamwork (with the sigil placed beneath a pillow or mattress) with the intent of weighing a decision, learning something of your own personal power or mental wellbeing, or with any questions you have about your career or confidence levels.

Be sure to jot any notes in your dream journal.

Week 22 - Ipos - Invocation/Evocation #1

Today, using the enn, invoke/evoke Ipos and work with him in one of the following areas:

1. Career
2. Confidence
3. Divination
4. Mental Well Being
5. Emotional Control
6. Personal Power
7. Decision Making

Week 22 - Ipos - Invocation/Evocation #2

Today, pick a different area and work with the Daemon on that. You can just do a standard request ritual, or you can do a full on Goetic evocation. The choice is yours.:

1. Career
2. Confidence
3. Divination
4. Mental Well Being
5. Emotional Control
6. Personal Power
7. Decision Making

Week 22 - Ipos - Create a Spell/Ritual

Create a spell or ritual for one of the following (feel free to share only if you want to):
1. To guide one to a career suited to the individual.
2. To become more confident.
3. For divination.
4. For mental well-being,
5. For stronger emotional control.
6. To tap personal power in the name of Ipos
7. To contact Ipos to help make a decision.

Week 22 – Ipos - Rest, Reflect, Meditate, Plan

How did your week with Ipos go? What did you learn? Did he give you direction/guidance? Ipos is a very versatile Daemonic force. Did you get this impression from him?

Make sure you write all of this down in your

journal. It will be useful for when you return to your journal at a later time.

WEEK 23: AIM

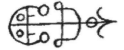

DUKE
Color: Green
Incense: Sandalwood
Metal: Copper
Planet: Venus
Element: Fire
Enn: Ayer avage secore Aim
Date: November 2 –12

Original Purpose: Makes one witty and gives true answers about people's private matters.

Author's Notes: The artists muse. Invoke Aim for creative inspiration or to find creative solutions to complex problems. Writers, artists and musicians should wear the sigil of Aim while working to prevent creative "blocks".

Week 23 – Aim - Meditation

Today, do you meditation like you normally do. Draw the sigil with colored pencils or even paints, but also feel free to draw or create anything that comes to mind during your meditation. If the inspiration strikes - create something from nothing.

Doodle stick figures. Play with color. Just go with the flow and see what comes of it.

Week 23 - Aim - Freewrite

Write down a list of your current problems. Then come up with creative solutions for each of them. Who cares if the solution you write out is ridiculous or completely unrealistic? Go with it. Let the free write take you in whatever direction it takes you.

Week 23 - Aim - Dreamwork

Do your dreamwork as usual. I don't have an exercise this time around just because I think Aim will lead you into what they think you need - even if it's just a good night's sleep. So how did you sleep?

Week 23 - Aim - Invocation/Evocation #1

Invoke/Evoke Aim using their enn and write out and burn a request for one of the following:

1. Creative inspiration.
2. Confidence
3. Better Communication with others or with the Daemonic.

4. Mental well-being.

Week 23 – Aim - Invocation/Evocation #2

Today, invoke/evoke Aim for a divination session with the Daemon. You can use a scrying mirror, pendulum session, or even an ascension or channeling (with automatic writing?). What comes of this session?

Week 23 - Aim - Create a Spell/Ritual

Create a spell or ritual for one of the following.

1. To find inspiration.
2. To uncover secrets.
3. To find opportunities.
4. For better communication.
5. To draw confidence.

Week 23 - Aim - Plan, Rest, Reflect, Meditate

How was this week for you overall? Did you find yourself more inspired? More confident? Is Aim a Daemon you vibe with? How satisfied, overall, are you with your work with Aim?

WEEK 24: NABERIUS

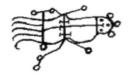

MARQUIS
Color: Violet
Incense: Jasmine
Metal: Silver
Planet: Moon
Element: Air
Enn: Eyan tasa volocur Naberius
Date: November 13 - 22

Original Purpose: Makes one cunning in arts and sciences and in rhetoric. Restores lost honor and dignity.

Author's Notes: Invoke Naberius for strength and guidance to do what is honorable and right even when you fear taking a stand for what you believe in. Naberius often makes magicians feel very *nervous*. This seems to be a natural effect of his energy. Consequently, he can infuse a magician with great courage and confidence.

Week 24 - Naberius - Meditation

There are so many areas Naberius can help you this week, and you don't have to try to focus on all of them. Just work with him as it aligns with your great work. Today, contemplate the sigil and the Daemonic force itself.

Just a brief list of areas he may be able to enlighten you this month:

- Arts & Sciences (Learning, Recall, Opportunities in these areas)
- Rhetoric/Communication (Especially persuading others)
- Honor & Dignity (Restoration of. Reconciliation would fall under this.)
- Strength/Courage
- Confidence
- Guidance (especially if you need help with your moral compass in an issue)

Be sure to write down any observations, interesting thoughts, images, or questions that arise from the meditative work.

Week 24 - Naberius - Freewrite

Today, look at the list of things Naberius does rather well from yesterday's exercise. In which of those areas can you use some reflection, inspiration, opportunity, advice? Write about this in your freewriting journal. Is there a topic that seems to keep coming up during the course of this class? If so, what can you do to change the situation to your will? How can Naberius help?

Week 24 - Naberius - Dreamwork

Using the method that works best for you - invite Naberius into your dreams with the intention of finding answers, strength, courage, confidence, or guidance on any issue he can help with. What comes of it?

Be sure to write anything you remember from the dream in your dream journal for later reflection.

Week 24 - Naberius - Invocation/Evocation #1

Today, invoke Naberius and do a standard Daemonolatry request burning ritual. It can be for any reason within Naberius' real of influence.

Some questions to consider in your journal: How did the energy in the room change? Note any and all sensory reactions you experienced. What did the Daemon feel like emotionally? And finally: What manifested from request burning? Leave a few lines so you can come back and fill it in later.

Week 24 - Naberius - Invocation/Evocation #2

Today, I want you to choose a divination device (crystal, scrying bowl, scrying mirror, pendulum) and vibrate the Daemon's enn over it until you feel the energy in the room and/or device change. Then I want you to perform a divination session.

You are welcome to write out your questions ahead of time and bring paper and pen into the session for you. This can also be performed as an astral ascension session if you prefer.

Week 24 - Naberius - Create a Spell or Ritual

This week, create a spell or ritual for one of the following:

- To obtain opportunities in the arts and sciences.

- To persuade others.

- To restore one's honor and/or friendships.

- To gain strength/courage/confidence.

- To guide the magician's moral compass.

Feel free to share your creation ONLY if you are comfortable doing so.

Week 24 - Naberius – Rest / Reflect / Meditate / Plan

Some questions you might ask yourself in your journal for this week's reflections:

How well did you vibe with Naberius? Did you have any profound spiritual revelations? Did the Daemon give you any self-work or suggest areas you could work on? Think back on the week and everything that happened. Which things potentially could have been influenced by Naberius?

As a note here - if you find a reflection question you like, you can add that question to your normal Sunday reflections, or create your own list of reflections. The whole point of the reflection day is for you to ask yourself questions about yourself in relation to the Daemonic, and how that manifested in your physical, mental, emotional, and spiritual life for the week.

WEEK 25: GLASYA-LABOLAS

Welcome to Week 25! You're almost 1/3 the way through the immersion!

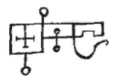

PRESIDENT
Color: Orange
Incense: Storax
Metal: Mercury
Planet: Mercury
Element: Fire
Enn: Elan tepar secore on ca Glasya-Lobolas.
Date: November 23 – December 2

Original Purpose: Teaches arts and sciences and creates wars and calamity. He teaches divination. He can make men invisible, and he can cause love between friends and foes.

Author's Notes: Also an Earl in some texts. Glasya Labolas can be invoked to keep what you're doing a secret from others. To make you 'invisible' per se. He can make you wise to what is really going on around you and can make your friends and enemies unsuspecting. You could certainly work with him for execration/binding, but also to keep projects secret from nosey co-workers or competitors or to keep a surprise party from a friend.

Week 25 - Glasya-Labolas - Meditation

Things to meditate on today as you draw the sigil and sit with it for a while:

How do you need to persuade others? How can you get over bad feelings toward others that may be holding you back? What do you need to know about the past that affects the present and influences the future?

Just think about these things today. Tomorrow, you'll write about them.

Week 25 - Glasya-Labolas - Freewrite

Today, I want you to write in your journal about situations that involve other people. How can you effectively influence the situation? In the case of people who have wronged you, what was your part in the situation? What should you keep hidden from others for the moment? This doesn't have to be a project or something nefarious, it could be something simple like hiding a surprise party from your best friend.
Some areas Glasya-Labolas can help in:

- Keeping projects/plans hidden.

- Influencing others.
- Divination.
- Find out what other people are doing behind your back, or learning their true feelings (if you're feeling brave).
- Execration/Binding
- Learning the arts and sciences.

You can adjust what questions (and answers) you have for yourself regarding all these areas, and this can help you discover in what areas of your life Glasya-Labolas can help you this week.

Week 25 - Glasya-Labolas - Dreamwork

Tonight, go into your dreamwork as usual with whatever you have decided to work with Glasya-Labolas for this week. Say or think his enn, your intent on getting insight into your personal situation, while also looking at the sigil.

What comes of this? Be sure to keep your dream journal handy so you can write down anything you remember as soon as you wake up.

Week 25 - Glasya-Labolas – Invocation / Evocation #1

Continue working on the situation you've decided to focus on for the week and either burn a request to the Daemon regarding the issue, do a divination session, or go into ascension.

Be sure to note your experience not only mentally and emotionally, but also physically.

Week 25 - Glasya-Labolas – Invocation / Evocation #2

Today I want you to specifically try a divination session. You can use the tool most suited to you. Whether it be a pendulum, tarot deck, or scrying device. Invoke Glasya-Labolas and ask him to preside over your divination session. Now, ask him what information you don't have that will help you move forward. See what answer you get.

Some of you will get very direct answers. Some of you will get answers you don't want to hear. Others will get archaic answers that don't make sense. Regardless the answer you get, write it down. Mull it over. Reflect on it. If you have any revelations about it, write this down, too. Remember - be honest with yourself. This is between you and the Daemonic Divine.

There may be a few among you who may choose this invocation to curse someone. If that's the case, remember not to have any guilt so you won't bring it back on yourself. Make sure a curse is really what you want to do. Also remember that you can curse situations and feelings, not just people. Cursing can be a great catalyst for healing in a lot of cases. Just make sure you don't hang onto it after you're done.

How did today's work go for you?

Week 25 - Glasya-Labolas - Create a Spell or Ritual

Today, I want you to create a spell or ritual working with Glasya-Labolas to affect one of the following areas:

- Execration/Binding
- Invisibility (i.e. keeping what you're doing hidden from others)
- See what others are hiding.
- Persuading Others
- Divination
- Learning the Arts and Sciences.

Week 25: Glasya-Labolas – Plan / Reflect / Rest / Meditate

How did this week go? Do you gain any insight? Did you vibe with Glasya-Labolas? Do you feel any of your magickal skills improving as we move forward? Do you feel your work with the Daemons so far has brought about any personal revelations or growth as you go through this shadow work? If not, how can you go a step deeper? Can you, perhaps, find something you fear in each Daemonic Force and face it going forward?

WEEK 26: BUNE

DUKE
Color: Green
Incense: Sandalwood
Metal: Copper
Planet: Venus
Element: Earth
Enn: (also Bime) – Wehlc melan avage Bune Tasa
Date: December 3 - 12

Original Purpose: He gives truthful answers, he can part the veil between the living and the dead and gather the dead. He can give riches and make a magician wise and well-spoken.

Author's Notes: Bune is one of the Goetia's Necromancy Daemons. If you have a medium ready to channel the dead, invoke Bune to keep order and peace during the séance. He can impart understanding and wisdom about the nature of death.

Week 26 - Bune - Meditation

Today I want you to draw the sigil of Bune and meditate on your or mortality or a life change. Hopefully this week will bring insight into one of these things, or both. When thinking of life changes think of everything from leaving school to enter the workforce. Marriage. New baby. New home. New city. Retirement. Divorce. Death of a loved one. All of these things are major life changes that can trigger stress, make us rethink our lives, or can cause us to grieve for what we're losing. And in some instances, spark excitement for the things we're gaining. Keep all of this in mind while moving ahead for the coming week.

Week 26 - Bune - Freewrite

Today, in your journal, I want you to explore your feelings and deepest emotions about change, death, and your own mortality. Which topic rises to the surface as an area to work on or meditate over this week? In what areas do you think Bune can help you? If none of this feels relevant, consider working with Bune for divination, general wisdom, or to speak to a deceased loved one via Necromancy.

Week 26 – Bune - Dreamwork

In tonight's dreamwork, visualize the seal of Bune

while drifting off to sleep (or recite his Enn) and go into sleep with the intent for Bune to offer his wisdom on death and change. What help can he offer you now?

Be sure to write anything that comes up immediately as you wake.

Week 26 - Bune - Invocation/Evocation #1

Today, I want you to invoke/evoke the Daemon and do a divination session. What wisdom comes of it?

Alternatives:
- Ascension Session
- Necromancy Session w/Spirit Board.

Week 26 - Bune - Invocation/Evocation #2

Today, invoke/evoke Bune and burn a request for wisdom or change (depending what you need). Sealing the request with a drop of your blood would be appropriate.

Leave space in your journal for later notes about the manifestation of this ritual, especially if it doesn't happen immediately.

Week 26 – Bune - Create a Spell or Ritual

Today, create a spell or ritual for one of the following:

- A ritual for necromancy.
- A ritual or spell for change.
- A divination spell or ritual utilizing Bune's influence.

Remember that these exercises are for inspiration only. If you have other ideas of what you'd like to do, do it. Experimentation is a great teacher.
Keep good notes on the ritual, and if you try it, the results.

Week 26 - Bune - Reflect/Rest/Meditate/Plan

How did your week with Bune go? Are you comfortable with the Death Daemonic? Did you have any revelations or experiences that stood out? Write this all in your journal.

WEEK 27: RONOVE

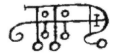

MARQUIS
Color: Violet
Incense: Jasmine
Metal: Silver
Planet: Moon
Element: Air
Enn: Kaymen vefa Ronove
Date: December 13 - 21

Original Purpose: Imparts the knowledge of tongues and favors of friends and foes. He also gives good servants and teaches rhetoric.

Author's Notes: The Daemon of knowledge and wisdom in the Dukanté Hierarchy. Ronove can also be invoked to cause people to see your way of thinking or feel the need to help you. Be careful of invoking Ronove to control others because it will often turn into a lesson for your benefit.

Week 27 - Ronove - Meditation

Today I want you to consider all of Ronove's areas of influence as you're meditating on the sigil.

Consider communication, confidence, knowledge, wisdom, and mental well-being. Also, consider glamour magick as well as divination and spirit communication. Looking at his correspondences, you'll also see these are areas where Ronove might excel in helping influence a situation for you.

One of the best offerings for Ronove is your time and effort. As a "teacher" Daemon, Ronove is also a go-to for a lot of students.

Week 27 – Ronove - Freewrite

Looking at yesterday's post, answer the following questions in your journal:

1. How can I best utilize Ronove's influence this week?

2. What do I need to know or learn in order to move forward?

3. In which areas of my life would confidence benefit me?

4. How can I better communicate with others?

Add additional questions and answers as you think of them, or just follow along where your train of thought leads you. Note any patterns in thinking that emerge. Note common themes. Look at the bigger picture.

Week 27 - Ronove - Dreamwork

Tonight, go into your dreamwork with the intention of getting answers on any issues that came up in your meditations and/or freewriting exercises.

Week 27 - Ronove - Invocation/Evocation #1

Invoke Ronove and burn a request for one of the following:

1. Help with concentration and studying.

2. To bring you more confidence.

3. To help you find the resources/tools to learn something new, get a certification, or go back to school.

4. Something not listed here.

Week 27 - Ronove - Invocation/Evocation #2

Hopefully by now, all of you have had the opportunity to read *Lake of Fire*, a book that teaches ascension.

Today I want all of you to invoke/evoke Ronove, and then do an ascension session with him. Pay particular attention to the space you end up in, and the images and things that pop into your head as you're doing this.

When finished, be sure to make detailed notes of the experience.

Some of you may choose to simply do a modified Goetic ritual to speak with Ronove in the black mirror.

Week 27 - Ronove - Create a Spell or Ritual

Please note that during these "create a spell or ritual" exercises, you are also welcome to create a magickal artifact, create a permanent sigil, paint, draw, compose music, or write. The point is that you create something every Saturday as your inspiration moves you. Of course, it's always fine to just meditate or do what you have the energy to do. Even if you just spend a week thinking about the Daemon, or glancing at its sigil every so often, that's fine.

Ideas for spells and rituals this week:

1. Create a glamour spell to bring you confidence no matter where you are. (This can also be an talisman

of some kind.)
2. Create a divination device enchanted in the name of Ronove.
3. Create a spell or ritual for better concentration and focus (for studying and learning).

Week 27- Ronove - Rest/Reflect/Meditate/Plan

What did your work with Ronove teach you this week? More specifically, what did Ronove teach you about yourself? About your communication? About your study style? About your confidence or mental well-being?

Write it up in your journal.

WEEK 28: BERITH

DUKE
Color: Green
Incense: Sandalwood
Metal: Copper
Planet: Venus
Element: Fire
Enn: Hoath redar ganabal Berith
Date: December 22 - 30

Original Purpose: Will give truthful answers. Can turn all metals to gold. He can give dignities. The original Goetia gives warning that Berith is a liar.

Author's Notes: Berith seems to prefer the magician to come to the correct answer on his own and will often impart mistruths to impart lessons. This seems to be a method of instruction rather than something done underhandedly. A Daemon of alchemy. Can teach the magician to help himself.

Week 28 - Berith - Meditation

Today as you meditate on Berith's seal, I want you to think of alchemical transformations within the self. We also hear rocks or metals into gold, but oftentimes, magicians take this literally. Think more along these lines: Turning pain and anger into productivity. Turning bad situations into a positive learning experience. Changing your frame of mind to alter the outcome of any situation.

Mind you, I'm not suggesting toxic positivity here. You should acknowledge the bad and feel all the emotions that come with it, but at the same time, you should always ask yourself: "What have I learned from this?" "Did anything good come of it?"

Can you see how every situation is a shade of gray? That all things negative may have a positive side and all positive things have a negative side?
Consider this along the philosophy of "All things are the same, just different degrees of the same." The situation doesn't change. It is what it is. But the degree to which you allow something to negatively or positively impact you dictates how "bad" the situation is.

Example: Imagine two people. Both of them have their car break down. It causes upheaval in both of their lives. Both of them will struggle to pay for the repair bill. Yet one of them takes it in stride, uses the experience to cull things from her schedule or walk more, and the situation doesn't seem nearly as bad as the same situation for the other person, who fights against the situation and reacts more emotionally to it, refusing to take the opportunity to rearrange things in a productive way. This is why some people's lives are constantly in chaos. They are constantly reacting to external situations, even fighting them, in a way that makes them struggle both internally and externally. Just consider this as food for thought while drawing Berith's seal.

Week 28 - Berith - Freewrite

Write about all the things you meditated on yesterday, or just write about ways in which Berith's attributes and wisdom may benefit you this week.

Week 28 – Berith - Dreamwork

Tonight, I want you to go into sleep/dreaming with the intention to learn something about yourself and how you can alchemize what's harmful into something productive. It can be a bad habit, a frequent disruptive emotion/feeling, or even a fear.

Week 28 - Berith - Invocation/Evocation #1

Today, I want you to try an exercise in alchemizing

what isn't useful into something that is.

Step 1: Invoke Berith

Step 2: Draw together (in your mind) all your angry, disappointed, sad, fearful, anxious thoughts and emotions.

Step 3: Visualize a cauldron in front of you. Hold your hands over it. Now visualize all those thoughts and emotions going from your head, through your shoulders and arms, and into the cauldron. If you feel yourself tensing as you do this, that's fine. Visualize it all leaving you and going into this cauldron.

Step 4: Now visualize Berith's energy pouring into the cauldron, changing sadness into optimism, anger into motivation, disappointment into resolve, fear into courage, and anxiety into serenity. Visualize the color of whatever you put into your cauldron changing with the addition of Berith's influence.

Step 5: Once everything in your visualized cauldron is "changed", draw the energy from the cauldron back into yourself. You're taking back all these emotions and thoughts, but in their CHANGED form.

Close the ritual.

MODIFICATION: For those of you who cannot visualize, I want you to think about each emotion and thought you want to change and think about what you would like them to be, then close your eyes and repeat Berith's enn in your head and ask him to change what is, to what could be in a more positive and productive way.

Be sure to write in your journal anything relevant to the ritual. How you felt, what you put in your cauldron, how it was changed and what it felt like to draw that changed energy back into you. Leave space so you can come back and write about what manifested from this ritual.

Week 28 - Berith - Invocation/Evocation #2

Today, invoke Berith (vibrating the enn until the energy in the room changes) and draw him into the ritual space. Write down what you hope to gain from working with him on a piece of paper. It could be:

1. Change - Turning rocks (counterproductive thoughts, emotions, habits) to gold (productive thoughts, emotions, habits).

2. Knowledge - Especially self-knowledge. Like understanding your own negative thought patterns or serial behavior that is counterproductive.

3. Helping Oneself - Finding resolve, or courage, to do what needs to be done to change something from a rock to gold.

4. Other. Whatever you wish to request from Berith.

Now, draw Berith's seal on the paper, add one drop of your blood (you can use menstrual blood, blood from a picked scab). If you are anti-bloodletting, just use another bodily fluid. Tears, sexual fluid, saliva, sweat. Now, burn the request in the offering bowl (to transfer it from the physical world to the infernal realm) and say, "So be it." Then close the ritual. (No, burning a sigil does not injure the Daemon. Fire is a process of transformation from one this world to another during a "request ritual".

Make a note of this invocation/evocation and leave space for notes on manifestation.

Or - do an invocation/evocation + ritual of your own.

Week 28 - Berith - Create a Spell or Ritual

Today, create a spell or ritual for one of the following:

1. Knowledge

2. Alchemy/Transformation

3. Self-help

4. Other

Week 28 - Berith - Plan/Rest/Reflect/Meditate

What did Berith teach you this week? Were you able to successfully turn your personal rocks into gold? Don't worry if you didn't. It takes practice. Be sure to write all of this in your notebook.

WEEK 29: ASTAROTH

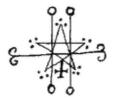

DUKE
Color: Green
Incense: Sandalwood
Metal: Copper
Planet: Venus
Element: Earth
Enn: Tasa Alora Foren Astaroth
Date: December 31 – January 9

Original Purpose: Can tell the truth and reveal all secrets. Can make men knowing of the liberal sciences and evidently knows the fall mythology (Milton's Paradise Lost) by heart.

Author's Notes: A Daemoness of Divination. Invoke her for scrying especially. She is also a Daemoness of friendship and love and can help you find these things.

Week 29 - Astaroth - Meditation

This is the week where I want those of you who are mediums/seers to practice your mirror, crystal, and fire scrying!

For those of you who aren't interested in vision magick and divination, concentrate on your friendships, lovers/partners, and/or self-love.
So, today, choose which area you'd like to focus on this week. You'll get more out of it if you focus, but if you want to meander around, you can do that, too. It's up to you.

Draw the seal and meditate on which area would most benefit you at this time.

Week 29 - Astaroth - Freewrite

For those of you who have chosen to work on friendship/love/self-love, write about that today.
For those of you who have chosen to work on your scrying skills - I want you to do a scrying session (without any Daemonic influence this time), and then write about the images, thoughts, and feelings that came to you. Try to do at minimum 5-10 minutes of scrying for this exercise.

Week 29 - Astaroth - Dreamwork

For those focusing on friendship, love, or self-love, go into tonight's sleep with the intention of gaining insight into these areas.

For those focusing on divination, focus on the sigil 5-10 minutes, then do a 5-10 minute scrying session -- THEN go to bed. See what happens. Do you dream? What is the dream about?

Be sure you're still keeping your dream notebook at your bedside with a working pen so you can write anything you remember of your dreams immediately upon waking.

Week 29 - Astaroth - Invocation/Evocation #1

Today, invoke/evoke Astaroth and then do a scrying session.

Advanced: Invoke/Evoke Astaroth. Bless a scrying mirror in the name of Astaroth or dedicate a scrying device in the name of Astaroth and then perform the scrying session.

Write up the ritual and what you saw, felt, heard during the session.

Week 29 - Astaroth - Invocation/Evocation #2

Repeat yesterday's invocation/evocation and scrying session. Does it come easier today? Did you get more information? Write up the similarities and differences. Write up all the information you received including visions, thoughts, feelings, sounds, smells, etc...

Week 29 - Astaroth - Create a Spell or Ritual

Today - Create a Spell or Ritual for one of the following:

1. To create an effective divination device (especially scrying mirrors/bowls/crystals in the name of Astaroth.
2. To draw self-love or love.
3. To draw friendship.
4. Other - whatever you choose.
You may also use Saturdays to create a permanent sigil, draw, paint etc... This is your Daemonolatry Arts & Crafts day.

Week 29 - Astaroth – Plan / Reflect / Rest / Meditate

Do you feel your scrying improved with a boost from Astaroth? How did you feel about Astaroth's energy? Did you vibe with it? What did Astaroth teach you about friendship, love, or self-love? Do you feel more confident in those areas after this week?

Write the answers to these questions and any others you can think of in your journal.

WEEK 30: FORNEUS

MARQUIS
Color: Violet
Incense: Jasmine
Metal: Silver
Planet: Moon
Element: Water
Enn: Senan okat ena Forneus ayer
Date: January 10 - 19

Original Purpose: Teaches rhetoric and languages. Gives men a good name and can cause one's enemies and friends to love him.

Author's Notes: Invoke Forneus to influence others to favor you. Invoke Forneus before legal battles to get favorable results.

Week 30 - Forneus - Meditation

So, Forneus has a lot of areas where his energy and instruction can benefit the magician. Just to make a quick list of them: career, confidence, glamour for influence or favor in the workplace, justice as in winning legal battles, execration magick, knowledge of foreign languages, and personal power. If you look at each thing individually it paints a different picture. But if you take it in all together - you can see that Forneus is great for career and work magick, as well as business. Anything to do with your job/career.

That said, he can help you analyze your work situation and overcome obstacles in that area (including problem co-workers).

So, as you're drawing and meditating on the sigil today, I want to you think about your work. If you're retired, unemployed, or a student - focus on a single area like confidence or personal power.
Note any thoughts this meditation provokes in your journal.

Week 30 - Forneus - Freewrite

Today I want you to write about your job, your confidence and sense of personal power, and any issues you might be experiencing here. It could be as simple as not being assertive enough. It could be as complex as being continually passed over for a contract, raise, or promotion. Or not being able to find a job that's a good fit.

Note any common themes in what you're telling yourself. What does this reveal? Answer this question in your journal.

Week 30 - Forneus - Dreamwork

Tonight, as you're looking at Forneus' seal as you're falling asleep, go into sleep with the intent to solve any issues that came up in your meditation or freewrite.

How is the dreamwork coming? Lucid dreaming and dream walking can be hard. Sometimes it will work, sometimes it won't. Don't beat yourself up if you're only getting results once in a while or half the time.

Week 30 - Forneus - Invocation/Evocation #1

Today, choose one of the following exercises. Invoke Forneus and:

1. Do a scrying session to get answers or wisdom for areas he can help in.
2. Perform a request ritual asking for help in an area he can help in.
3. Draw the energy of Forneus into you to increase confidence and to find your inner power.

Week 30 - Forneus - Invocation/Evocation #2

Choose a different one from the list for today:
Invoke Forneus and:
1. Do a scrying session to get answers or wisdom for

areas he can help in.

2. Perform a request ritual asking for help in an area he can help in.

3. Draw the energy of Forneus into you to increase confidence and to find your inner power.

Week 30 - Forneus - Create a Talisman

You see what I did there? I just switched things up. You can still create a spell or ritual this week if you prefer, but today I want you to create a talisman or sigil to invoke your personal power or confidence. Make it out of any material you like and consecrate it to Forneus.

Week 30 - Forneus - Plan/Rest/Reflect/Meditate

What was your takeaway from working with Forneus? What did you learn about yourself? What was your favorite part of the week? What was your least favorite part?

Write this in your journal.

WEEK 31: FORAS

PRESIDENT
Color: Orange
Incense: Storax
Metal: Mercury
Planet: Mercury
Element: Earth
Enn: Kaymen vefa Foras
Date: January 20 -29

Original Purpose: Knowledge of herbs and stones. Teaches logic and ethics and helps men live long and in good health. Can give treasure and find lost items.

Author's Notes: Seek Foras to solve problems, especially those of a business nature. Foras gives stability and a clear head.

Week 31 - Foras - Meditation

In today's meditation I want you, while you're focusing on Foras' sigil, to consider your creativity and how that relates to your mental well-being. Are you giving yourself enough creative time? Are you

143

taking care of yourself? Are you setting boundaries with others in relation to your time? What is essential to your mental well-being? What wisdom and knowledge do you need?

Week 31 - Foras - Freewrite

Today in your journal - write down your answers to the questions you contemplated yesterday during your meditation. Are you giving yourself enough creative time? Are you taking care of yourself? Are you setting boundaries with others in relation to your time? What is essential to your mental well-being? What wisdom and knowledge do you need?

Now let's look at what Foras excels at:
1. The business side of careers. Like paperwork, taxes, licenses, etc.
2. Creativity - especially if you work in a creative career!
3. Knowledge (of business, business-sense)
4. Mental Well-Being (creativity)
5. Wisdom (in business)

So, Foras is actually a great Daemon to work with if you are in a creative career, because you need solid business sense. At the same time, you can work with him for each of the above things individually.

Week 31 - Foras - Dreamwork

Tonight as you establish your intent before going to sleep, consider all the things Foras might be able to help you with this week. What wisdom do you need from Foras? Go into sleep seeking this wisdom.

Week 31 - Foras - Invocation/Evocation #1

For today's invocation, I want you to Invoke/evoke Foras and once you feel the energy in the room change, work on a creative project, or simply bask in Foras' energy and "feel it out".

Week 31 - Foras - Invocation/Evocation #2

Today, after you Invoke/Evoke Foras, either repeat yesterday's exercise as your mood dictates, or choose to do a scrying ritual with Foras (spirit communication) or a request ritual.

Don't forget to write your experiences up in your journal. Even if it's just a brief note, "Did XYZ work with Daemon today."

Week 31 - Foras - Create a Spell or Ritual

Today, create a spell or ritual for one of the following (or just meditate or create a new art piece or something:

1. An talisman for opportunities to learn new skills with the help of Foras.
2. A creativity charm infused with Foras energy.
3. A ritual with Foras for serenity and mental-well being - maybe a calming meditation?
4. A ritual to draw the wisdom and knowledge of Foras.

Or create something from scratch! Remember that these are just suggestions for exercises and you're free to work with each Daemon as you wish.

Week 31 - Foras - Rest/Reflect/Plan/Meditate

In your journal, answer the following questions: Did you find this week a bit more relaxing? Were you able to get in touch with a creative part of yourself? Did Foras' energy bring you a sense of well-being? Did you learn something new about your business or business plan (if this applies to you). How did Foras help you? What did you learn about yourself?

WEEK 32: ASMODAY

KING
Color: Yellow
Incense: Frankincense
Metal: Gold
Planet: Sun
Element: Air
Enn: Ayer avage Aloren Asmoday aken
Date: January 30 – February 8

Original Purpose: He is keeper of the ring of virtues and can give said ring. He can lead the magician to treasure, make him invincible, and will give true answers to demands. He also teaches mathematics, astronomy and crafts.

Author's Notes: Some believe Asmoday is one of three the three heads (the others being Amaymon and Amducius) in the Asmodai image in Collin DePlancy's *Dictionnaire Infernal*. Some believe Asmoday is equal to Asmodeus, a Daemon of lust and passion. Asmoday can be worked with to make the magician physically stronger and mentally sharp. See the section on the Asmodai at the end of the book to learn more.

Week 32 - Asmoday - Meditation

Today, I would like you to draw the seal and sit quietly with it, thinking of truth and honesty, or strength and wisdom. If you have any creative impulses during this meditation either act on them, or write them down afterward. What feelings does Asmoday bring you? If you need advice on anything, what would your inner-Asmoday give you for advice?

Week 32 - Asmoday - Freewrite

During today's freewrite, I want you to write about your authentic self. Are you being true to yourself and honest with others? Are you fully tapping your inner strength to deal with any struggles you're currently facing? What questions in these areas are facing you now? For some of you, none of these areas may apply. If not, consider what Asmoday may inspire you to. In the Goetia, he is the keeper of the ring of virtues, which he can give to the magician. But he can also teach you to create your own talismans. All of the Asmodai deal with areas of passion, creativity, and inspiration. What is your passion? What do you wish to create for yourself and/or others? What inspires you?

Week 32 - Asmoday - Dreamwork

When you settle into tonight's dreamwork, visualize the sigil, think the enn if you wish, and go into sleep, try focusing on one area where you could use Asmoday's wisdom. Try to remember any dreams and be sure to make a note of the quality of your sleep. I think this is important to do after every dreamwork session because it may give you insight into which Daemonic forces lull you into deeper states of sleep and which ones keep you up at night so you can identify potential patterns later on.

Week 32 - Asmoday - Invocation/Evocation #1

Construct your ritual space as you see fit and call on Asmoday from the center of the space using the enn. Chant or vibrate the enn until the energy in the room changes. Today, I just want you to bask in that changed energy space for a while. Sit with it. Note how Asmoday's energy feels against your skin. Does it have a taste, a smell, an emotion? Does it make you feel invigorated? Contemplative? Don't do anything else. You don't need to grovel or leave offerings today. Just sit with him like you might an old friend while enjoying a cup of tea or coffee. Simply feel one another out and enjoy Asmoday's company. If you have any ideas, revelations, or any other notable inspirations - jot them in your journal.

Week 32 - Asmoday - Invocation/Evocation #2

Yesterday, I asked you to merely sit with Asmoday's energy, and this is something you can do with any Daemonic force when you're first meeting or feeling one another out. Today, however, I want you to choose one of the following for your invocation. Follow the same instructions by constructing your ritual space, vibrating the enn until the energy in the room changes, and then:

1. Write a request for advice, inspiration, strength on a slip of paper and burn it in the offering bowl. (Adding a drop of your blood to the paper is a traditional practice if you're not squeamish about blood magick.)
2. If you're an artist, crafter, writer, poet, or musician - ask Asmoday to inspire you and then create something (even a rough sketch or draft).
3. Bless or consecrate and talisman or ritual object to Asmoday.
4. Do whatever you like or simply repeat yesterday's exercise. Not all our time spent with the Daemonic needs to be active, or asking for things, or thanking them. Sometimes we need to just spend some time with them, doing absolutely nothing except enjoying one another's presence.

Week 32 - Asmoday - Create a Spell or Ritual

Instead of a spell or ritual today, I want you to

create some kind of sigil, talisman, or even an invocation for one or more of the following:

1.Inspiration
2. Strength
3. Honesty (in ourselves and others)
4. Honest advice or wisdom.
5. An aid to help one focus their studies in the sciences.

Week 32 - Asmoday – Rest /Reflect /Plan/ Meditate

What did Asmoday teach you about your authentic self this week? What wisdom or honest answers did you receive from Asmoday? Did Asmoday inspire you? How are your energy levels a week into working with him? How focused did you feel throughout the week? Write these answers in your journal.

WEEK 33 - GAAP

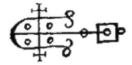

PRESIDENT
Color: Orange
Incense: Storax
Metal: Mercury
Planet: Mercury
Element: Air
Enn: Deyan Anay Tasa Gaap
Date: February 9 - 18

Original Purpose: He can steal other mages familiars and give them to you. He has the power to render men ignorant or to give them great wisdom and knowledge. He can teach you to consecrate things in the name of Amaymon. He can move people from one kingdom to another. He also seems to teach philosophy, liberal science, can cause both love and hatred, and tell you anything you want to know.

Author's Notes: Also listed as a Prince. Invoke Gaap to render others' magick or power inert while enhancing your own.

Week 33 - Gaap - Meditation

One thing you'll notice about a lot of the Goetic spirits is that their purposes overlap, so you'll find that working through the Goetia, you'll come back to the same situations/issues over and over again, just from different angles. There are plenty of opportunities to use this class to work on your divination skills, as well as self-confidence and personal power. So, if any of this feels repetitive, just remember that you're looking at the same situation - just from a different angle.

Some things Gaap can help you with include: Ignorance/Knowledge, Travel Opportunities, Divination, Protection, and power over people and/or situations that wish you harm or are holding you back. He's especially useful in teaching us how to learn how much of our power we GIVE to others willingly. How much we allow other people's offhanded comments, or unsolicited (or solicited) opinions to influence our own decisions. Now, sometimes it's great to take the advice of others when it helps us to level up or get where we want to be. But sadly, so many of us listen to the naysayers and the people who want to hold us back.

So, this week is about learning discernment in this area and protecting ourselves from this sort of thing, and really learning to understand what we control vs. What others actually control. The answer there is obviously - you control what you do, and let others control what they do — but don't allow them to control you.

A good example here is if we saddle others with the responsibility for our happiness and success, then we're giving them the power over our happiness and success. No one else is responsible for your happiness and success except you. Some people seek to shirk that responsibility.

As you're drawing the sigil and meditating on Gaap today, I want you to think about all of this.

Week 33 - Gaap - Freewrite

From yesterday's meditation, now that you've had time to mull over all your thoughts on the matter, write down what you learned about yourself, your personal responsibility, and what power you may be giving to others (sometimes even unknowingly until it's pointed out to us). Did you find anything disturbing? Are you ready to take action to change this? And if none of this applies, maybe it's time to write down all the places you want to travel or set some divination goals for the week. Or consider doing a spiritual house cleaning and protection over your dominion. Write down your thoughts on all of this. It will give you something to think about in the coming week when you actually start working with the Daemon.

Week 33 - Gaap - Dreamwork

Tonight, go into your dreamwork with the intention of learning something you didn't know before, or protecting yourself psychically, or even taking your power back from a person or situation. Again, jot any dreams you remembered, or any thoughts or feelings you had upon waking in your dream journal. For those of you working on spirit communication, you can always go into your dreamwork with the intention of speaking with the Daemon seeking wisdom and knowledge for what you need to know now, at this time in your life.

Week 33 - Gaap - Invocation/Evocation #1

During today's invocation, I'd like you to do one of the following:

1. Burn a request.
2. Curse a bad situation, or a person who has been holding you back.
3. Do a spirit communication (ascension) or divination session with the Daemon.
4. Ask the Daemon to bring you opportunities for travel.
5. Ask the Daemon to protect your home and person from attacks from others.

Week 33- Gaap - Invocation/Evocation #2

Today, choose a different one:

1. Burn a request.
2. Curse a bad situation, or a person who has been holding you back.
3. Do a spirit communication (ascension) or divination session with the Daemon.
4. Ask the Daemon to bring you opportunities for travel.
5. Ask the Daemon to protect your home and person from attacks from others.

Week 33 - Gaap - Create a Spell or Ritual

Today, create a spell or ritual (or a magickal talisman) for one of the following:
1. Protection
2. Draw opportunity for travel.
3. Power over others.
4. To consecrate a divination device in the name of Gaap.

Week 33 - Gaap - Rest/Reflect/Plan/Meditate

What did you learn from your week with Gaap? Don't worry if you feel like you've learned little from a week. There are a lot of reasons why some weeks will be more profound than others. Sometimes we really don't connect with a specific force. Other times we connect deeply. Sometimes we're just too busy and our hearts aren't into it. Other weeks we're fully present. All of this is okay. That's life and the Daemonic understands far more than some will give them credit. What's your takeaway from the week? Is there anything you'll be more mindful of going forward? Answer all of this, and your own questions, in your journal.

WEEK 34: FURFUR

EARL
Color: Red
Incense: Dragon's Blood
Metal: Copper or Silver
Planet: Mars
Element: Fire
Enn: Ganen menach tasa Furfur
Date: February 19 - 28

Original Purpose: A lord of storms, he can spark love between men and women. He can answer questions about the secret and the divine. Allegedly he won't speak the truth unless compelled.

Author's Notes: Invoke Furfur to raise energy during a ritual or before. Furfur is the Daemon of fire scrying. It's not that he won't speak the truth but rather you have to ask the right question and he will tell you whatever you want to know.

Week 34 - Furfur - Meditation

Furfur is a Daemonic force for energy work, raising emotional storms, love magick, fire scrying, and discovering hidden divine knowledge. Of course, his purposes may not stop there, but the only way to truly know how he can help you is to work with him. After drawing out the sigil in contemplation, if the weather permits in your area, I recommend doing this meditation in front of a fire (or a candle, weather not permitting). Simply gaze gently into the flame while visualizing the sigil you just drew. Be sure to note any random thoughts, feelings, images that came to mind during the session. During any meditation, be sure to start by focusing on the breath. It is always the breath you can come back to if you find your mind wandering to mundane things like emptying the dishwasher. That said, don't be so sure that emptying the dishwasher is just a mundane thought. Sometimes insight and clarity come to us when we're doing mundane tasks like housework, showering, driving.

Week 34 - Furfur- Freewrite

Today, write about your meditation. Write about things you've thought about Furfur or the areas in which he is said to preside. Consider which of his areas of expertise might be useful to you now. Also note your energy levels and if you can, record them throughout the day, noting any dips or surges. Being mindful of your natural energy rhythms and where you're conserving or exerting energy may be just the information you need to help you with future path and shadow work.

Week 34 - Furfur - Dreamwork

Tonight, I want you to go into the dream world with the intent of discovering ways to boost your energy or make the most of nervous energy. You're also welcome to go into sleep with other intentions. Like working on love and relationships or gaining knowledge that will help you in your spiritual journey. Sometimes visualizing the sigil and thinking the enn as you're falling asleep can be beneficial in helping you into a lucid dreaming/or astral travel state.

Week 34 - Furfur - Invocation/Evocation #1

People often view invocation/evocation as an opportunity to request or ask for something. Or to do a spell or draw a certain type of energy. But today and tomorrow I want you to try at least one of the following:

1. Invoke the Daemon by vibrating the enn until the energy in the room changes, visualize the Daemonic energy flowing into you, then try the suggested energy work exercise below.
2. Invoke the Daemon by vibrating the enn until the energy in the room changes, and then do a fire

scrying session.

ENERGY EXERCISE:

Place a lit candle before you and sit comfortably in front of the candle. You can even sit at a table for this exercise if you wish. Rub your hands together vigorously until they're hot, and then draw your hands apart about 6-8 inches, palms facing one another. Visualize a glowing red ball of energy building between your palms. Upon that ball of energy, visualize Furfur's sigil. Do this until you can almost feel the ball of energy. If you try to bring your hands together, you should feel some resistance. Now, lift that energy ball above the flame of the candle. Note the flame's reaction. Draw the ball to the right. Does the flame follow? Draw the ball to the left. What happens then? Drop the ball onto the flame and see what happens. If you have a yard and a piece of metal, you might try the energy ball exercise outdoors, but instead of attempting to manipulate the candle flame - try throwing the fireball you create at your metal object (which should be 3-6 feet in front of you) and see if anything happens. How does your personal energy level feel after these exercises?

Please note that drawing Daemonic energy into you can result in unwanted possession, or a productive channeling session depending on your skill level and mediumship ability. If this happens, try some automatic writing and see what happens.

Week 34 - Furfur - Invocation/Evocation #2

Today, look at yesterday's invocation/evocation exercise and either repeat, or choose a different activity. As always, you're welcome to do your own thing, or even try these exercises in the astral temple as necessary.

Week 34 - Furfur - Create a Spell or Ritual

Create a spell or ritual with Furfur for one of the following:

1. To draw energy into you.
2. A fire scrying spell/ritual
3. A spell to find true love or to add spark to a relationship.
4. A spell or ritual to help you discover divine truth.

Remember that your own spells and rituals have the most power, and it is in the nature of every magician to create. So, with every ritual or spell you create, you're creating a personal link with that Daemonic force. Feel free to use other books with spells and rituals as inspiration for your own. Modify or change things. Experiment and have fun with this exercise. By the time this class is finished, you should have your own working grimoire with anything you need (provided you're doing these exercises).

Week 34 - Furfur - Rest/Reflect/Plan/Meditate

What did you learn about your energy this week? What activities, thoughts, situations, people are you giving your energy to, and are you benefiting from this? What could change? Have you considered ways to alchemize negative energy into something positive for you? Think about this. What other things did your work with Furfur teach you? I always recommend leaving a little blank space after every journal entry, so you can go back later and jot additional notes.

WEEK 35: MARCHOSIAS

MARQUIS
Color: Violet
Incense: Jasmine
Metal: Silver
Planet: Moon
Element: Fire
Enn: Es na ayer Marchosias Secore
Date: March 1 - 10

Original Purpose: A warrior.

Author's Notes: Marchosias can teach discipline and coping skills. He can be invoked that the magician may learn to control his own temper and wield it as a warrior might his sword. Seek Marchosias for confidence, courage, and strength.

Week 35 - Marchosias - Meditation

Marchosias is one of those "career" Daemons in the sense that he works with the magician's ambition to help the magician manifest what he wants in the career-identity part of a magician's life. In this sense, he can instill career confidence, emotional and mental well-being - and can also keep you protected from office politics and workplace bullies, while doling out a bit of vengeance or justice as necessary. I actually have a friend who keeps the sigil of Marchosias framed on her office wall for all to see and has since she first started at the company. Now, she's the VP of marketing. But Marchosias isn't just for white collar corporate types, or even people who work at all. Wherever the magician has AMBITION, this is where Marchosias' influences are. If you have the ambition to build miniature houses and enter them in competitions, Marchosias can help. So today, while you're drawing the sigil and sitting with it, I want you to think about everything you're ambitious about. Even if you think it's something silly like home-improvement (hey, some of us are ambitious about such things).

Note: If you find yourself getting bored with the schedule, feel free to mix it up a little with your own self-created exercises. I decided to stick to a schedule because it facilitates discipline, and some people really need that. I figured the self-starters/motivators would likely tend toward doing their own thing anyway. :)

Week 35 - Marchosias - Freewrite

Today, write about your ambitions. What do you hope to achieve? What gets you motivated? What projects, ideas, or events are you motivated to give your energy to? Why? What does this tell you about yourself?

There's always one person doing this exercise who feels like nothing motivates them or that they have no ambitions. If you're this person, take a step back. What motivates you to get out of bed in the morning? Maybe it's time to take a look at life and see what you can change to make things better. If you don't have ambitions now, what were your ambitions when you were younger? Did you accomplish them? If you aren't feeling ambitious, what's changed in life? Just explore these questions and see what comes out of your brain.

Week 35 - Marchosias - Dreamwork

Tonight, I want you to go into the dream with the intent to have the Daemon give you wisdom on your Great Work. What is your Great Work? What is your life's calling? What task are you always called on to do, even if you try to walk away from it? Sometimes our great work seems counter-intuitive or like it's not really what we're supposed to be doing until we realize it is. I, for example, was in denial about my Great Work for years. After all, how could my great work be to inspire and teach others? Once I accepted that was my Great Work, it all fell into place. What wisdom does Marchosias have to offer to you about this?

Week 35 - Marchosias - Invocation/Evocation #1

For this week's Invocation/Evocation (both #1 and #2), I want you to choose one of the following:

1. Draw the Daemon into your ritual space and then into you for the purpose of mental well-being.

2. Do a divination and ask about your career or your Great Work.

3. Burn a request for protection or justice. Or even an opportunity.

4. Do your own thing. Listen to your intuition.

Week 35 - Marchosias - Invocation/Evocation #2

Choose a different one from the list today:

1. Draw the Daemon into your ritual space and then into you for the purpose of mental well-being.

2. Do a divination and ask about your career or your Great Work.

3. Burn a request for protection or justice. Or even an opportunity

4. Do your own thing. Listen to your intuition.

Week 35 - Marchosias - Create a Spell or Ritual

Today, create a spell or ritual for:

1. Career opportunities.
2. To discover your Great Work.
3. A protection charm.
4. Vengeance.
5. Mental well-being.
6. A confidence charm.

Week 35 - Marchosias – Rest /Reflect /Plan /Meditate

What wisdom did Marchosias offer you this week? Did you learn something you didn't know? How did the Daemon's energy feel combined with yours? Did you find Marchosias comfortable to work with?

WEEK 36: STOLAS

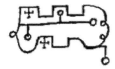

PRINCE
Color: Blue
Incense: Cedar
Metal: Tin
Planet: Jupiter
Element: Air
Enn: (also Stolos)– Stolos Ramec viasa on ca
Date: March 11 -20

Original Purpose: Teaches astronomy and the properties of herbs and stones.

Author's Notes: Stolas is another "teacher" Daemon. Invoke him to learn witchcraft or sciences of the natural world (i.e. biology, geology, botany, etc..). Wear an talisman of his sigil (can be made of clay or wood as well as Tin) while learning of these things and you will retain more information and attune yourself with the natural world.

Week 36 - Stolas - Meditation

This week, while drawing Stolas' sigil, visualize

yourself sitting in a meadow, or a forest, or on the beach. It doesn't matter as long as it's in nature. If you can do this exercise outdoors, all the better. Feel the breeze. Listen to the sounds of the birds and the plants. Listen to the ocean. Find your center. Breathe deeply. When you're ready, press your hands into the ground and feel your connection with the natural world. Sit with this for as long as you wish. You've also imbued the seal with this feeling. This connectedness. During the meditation, if you find your mind wandering, come back to the breath and your connectedness to nature.

Week 36 - Stolas- Freewrite

This week's freewriting exercise is a little more thought provoking. Spend a few minutes writing out your contemplation of your place in all that is. When do you feel most connected to nature? When don't you? When you slow down, balance and ground yourself, do you notice your mind clearing? How essential is it that you get out of your mundane life and reconnect? Do you feel refreshed and ready to take on whatever comes your way? While Stolas is an Airy Daemon, the point of his purpose is to teach and for the magician to learn. But reconnecting to the natural world opens our minds and intellect to receive the information he has to impart. How do you feel about that? In what ways can this help you now, in your present position?

Week 36 - Stolas - Dreamwork

Tonight, I want you to go into your dreamwork with the intent to learn. As you're drifting to sleep, visualize the sigil, or the Daemon (you may employ the enn or use your own invocation), and let sleep take you. Visualize yourself talking to the Daemon. How does he look? Smell? Sound? Listen to what he has to tell you.

Immediately upon waking, grab your journal and write down everything you remember. If you remember nothing, that's okay. It may come to you during your day. Do note how you felt the day after this dreamwork session. Did any wisdom come to you? Did you notice a pretty rock and feel the urge to pick it up, or find a flower you wanted to smell or pluck from the ground? Either take a photo of it, or pick up the rock. Listen to your gut.

Week 36 - Stolas - Invocation/Evocation #1

Consider trying one of the following exercises during today's invocation.

1. Call Stolas and do an elemental balancing and meditation.
2. Call Stolas and do a divination session.
3. Draw Stolas into your ritual space and bring with you several stones or crystals. Feel their energies

and write down the immediate feeling you get from them, then remember which was which and try using them in spells and rituals later on for rituals where you may want to invoke that feeling or purpose you got off of the stone.

Remember that you're welcome to do your own thing, or even perform a proper Goetic ritual if you wish. I want this immersion to be accessible to magicians of all ability levels, schools of magickal thought, and time limitations or excesses. Let the Daemonic flow around you, certainly, but let it flow through you. Remember that you, too, are part of the divine and each Daemonic force dwells within as well as without.

Week 36 - Stolas - Invocation/Evocation #2

Today, consider trying one of the following exercises:

1. Call on Stolas and ask for a clear mind and clear focus.
2. Call on Stolas and seek his tutelage on matters concerning the natural world. He can guide you provided you listen to that inner voice. That inner Stolas if you will.
3. Call on Stolas and seek inspiration in his divine presence.

Week 36 - Stolas - Create a Spell or Ritual

Today, act on any inspiration for the week. Just let your intuition reign supreme. Write a spell or ritual for anything that you are inspired to write it for. Create. Make your ritual grand and full of oration. Or make it simple. Create a talisman for anything. The key is to allow the Daemon's wisdom inspire you to magick that is of your own creation. (Maybe with some of his input.)

Week 36 - Stolas - Rest/Reflect/Plan/Meditate

What did Stolas teach you this week? Were you inspired? Did you experience visions? Do you feel more clarity? More balance? More in tune with your intuition? Be sure to write down anything you may have forgotten to record during your week. As always, if all you were able to do was reflect on the Daemons sigil all week (or carry it with you), that's okay. Don't beat yourself up if you missed a day of workings or if you found yourself doing the minimal work. Some weeks you'll have more time and energy than others, and you have to work with that.

WEEK 37: PHENEX

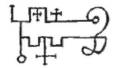

MARQUIS
Color: Violet
Incense: Jasmine
Metal: Silver
Planet: Moon
Element: Fire
Enn: (also Phenix, Pheynix, Phoenix)– Ef enay Phenex ayer
Date: March 21 - 30

Original Purpose: He is a poet and loves to discuss science (evidently).

Author's Notes: Another Daemonic muse for the creative. Invoke Phenex during Fire baptisms and rebirth rituals including creative path working.

Week 37 - Phenex - Meditation

Phenex is best known as a Daemon for transformation, but Phenex also rules over creativity (actually doing the creative thing), divination, intuitive knowledge, and communication of these things. Sometimes spirit communication comes into play here, too. Especially in clairsentience and being able to decipher and act on the images, thoughts, and feelings sent to us, as well as being able to articulate them. So today, while you're drawing the sigil, I want you to allow the visualization of the sigil engulf you in its flames and see what comes of it. What thoughts suddenly occur? What are you immediately spurred to act on? Hey - even if it's acting on an urge to clean something - it counts.

Week 37 - Phenex - Freewrite

Today I want you to think about all the things you've been putting off DOING. It could be simple like giving the dog a bath. Or it could be complex, like changing your entire career and moving to a new city. If each day is a fresh start, what can you start doing today that could ultimately transform your life in the long term? Choose one small thing. If you stopped putting this one small thing off, what would you gain from it a month from now? Six months? A year? Five years? Ten years?

Week 37 - Phenex - Dreamwork

Tonight, as you fall asleep, I want you to visualize yourself as a bird flying toward the Sun. As you get closer, you become a flame. As you become a flame, you burn more and more brightly. Now allow yourself to glide back to the Earth, gently, back into your bed. Your flames have been extinguished; you are ashes. From those ashes, you become solid and a new you emerges. If you can remember what the new you looked like, felt like, and how (s)he was different - be sure to note that, along with any remembered dreams you had, in your dream journal in the morning.

Week 37 - Phenex - Invocation/Evocation #1

Today, I want you to do a rebirth ritual as your Invocation/Evocation. You can do it in the astral temple, or just visualize it in your mind's eye if you don't have the space or time to do a physical ritual.

It's easiest to do this ritual in the nude. Start by evoking/invoking Phenex by vibrating the Daemon's enn until the energy in the room changes. Draw the Daemon's sigil on a piece of paper. Prick your finger and add a drop of blood. Burn the sigil in the offering bowl while thinking of your own transformation into a stronger, better, more confident, creative, disciplined (whatever it is) you, and visualize that sigil rising to the Daemonic plane and being captured by Phenex (as they connect to you). Let the flame consume the sigil to ash. Now, use the ash to draw the seal of Phenex on your body (anywhere). Rub some ash into your third eye. Now raise your hands high above you.

"Who I am is no more. My prior habits are no more.

I have flown to the Sun and been burnt to cinders. I fell like ash back to the Earth. Yet from these ashes I rise, rise, rise!"

Visualize what the new you looks like (and it doesn't have to look much different, except, for example, the new you isn't a smoker.) Take three deep breaths.

Visualize yourself taking shape and rising, your light (aura) shining.

Some people might call this an exercise in boosting your ego. I call it an exercise in finding inner strength and exerting your will in such a way that it sends a flood of endorphins into your blood stream. It's a lot easier to make a change if we can connect it to a powerful, wonderful feeling. Consider this.

Once you're finished with the ritual, thank Phenex for his presence and resume your day. I do see this as a morning ritual if you're a morning person, but for some of you it may be better suited as a night ritual. You might try it both in the morning and in the evening to see if the effect is different. Remember, part of being a magician is being willing to experiment and try new things or add creative twists. Once you learn the rules, feel free to break "the rules" in meaningful (to you) ways.

Week 37 - Phenex - Invocation/Evocation #2

Today, what you do with your invocation/evocation is your choice, but I highly recommend either doing some artwork with Phenex lending his energy to whatever you're drawing, painting, or creating, or doing a divination session with Phenex

Week 37 - Phenex - Create a Spell or Ritual

Create a Spell or Ritual (or a magickal artifact) for one of the following:

1. To spark motivation to act in the name of Phenex.
2. To bless a divination device in the name of Phenex.
3. To speak to the muses.
4. To transform the self.
5. To heighten intuition.

Week 37 - Phenex - Rest/Reflect/Plan/Meditate

What became clear to you during your work with Phenex? Did you find a hidden motivator? Did you see areas where transformation will benefit you? How did Phenex's energy mesh with your own?

Could you see yourself working with Phenex again?
Answer these questions in your journal.

WEEK 38: HALPHAS

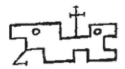

EARL
Color: Red
Incense: Dragon's Blood
Metal: Copper or Silver
Planet: Mars
Element: Air (Fire)
Enn: Erato Halphas on ca secore
Date: March 31 – April 10

Original Purpose: He builds armies and fortifications, arms them, and tells them what to do.

Author's Notes: Invoke Halphas to gather your allies and draw friends. Seek Halphas' wisdom in social situations where group mechanics are at play. Wear the sigil of Halphas to be well received and to command respect by those around you. Halphas is a good Daemon for Supervisors and Managers to work with to gain wisdom on how to lead.

Week 38 - Halphas - Meditation

Halphas is a good leadership coach. He can help you figure out self-sabotaging habits and fears and ways to overcome them. He can help you find your inner confidence and organization to lead. He can help you go over your life and find the areas you SHOULD be concentrating on, instead of areas where you might be wasting time. If there were a team of Daemons on a committee to help you find and pursue your great work - Halphas would be on that committee. For today's meditation - just draw the sigil in your journal, then think about how the lines and the visual aesthetic of the sigil makes you feel. Contemplate all the areas of influence Halphas rules over. He also rules over friendship, justice, and protection.

Week 38 - Halphas - Freewrite

How would you rate your leadership skills? What is the health of your friendships? Do you need to reinforce your wards or do any protections on yourself or your property? What are you focused on that you don't need to be as focused on? What would having more confidence do for you? Could Halphas help you when it comes to networking for your career and/or hobbies and passions? What would your inner Halphas say about your ability to lead your life? Your family? Your career? Do you need justice? Answer these questions in your freewrite journal.

Week 38 - Halphas - Dreamwork

Tonight, just go into sleep visualizing Halphas' sigil and with the intent to seek wisdom. When you wake - do you remember any dreams? Any details that stand out? How was the quality of your sleep? Do you feel refreshed? Tired? Irritated? Happy? Sad? Write all of this down in your dream journal.

Week 38 - Halphas - Invocation/Evocation #1

Today, write YOUR OWN invocation to Halphas. It can incorporate the Enn. Once the energy in the room changes, choose one of the following:

1. Meditation in Halphas' presence. Be sure to write down any thoughts or ideas that come during the meditation.
2. Burn a request to Halphas.
3. Ask Halphas to protect your home and visualize a barrier made of a bright red or silver light around your home or property. You can visualize his seal on the barrier.

Week 38 - Halphas - Invocation/Evocation #2

Today, vibrate the Enn of Halphas until the energy

in the room changes, then do one of the following:

1. Visualize yourself leading a project, a job, or a group.
2. Visualize friends all around you, supporting you and you supporting them.
3. Draw Halphas' energy into you to boost confidence and make areas where you need work more apparent.

Week 38 - Halphas - Create a Spell or Ritual

Today I'd like you to create a spell, ritual, or magickal artifact for one of the following in the name of Halphas:

1. A confidence spell, ritual, or talisman.
2. A spell or ritual to draw friends.
3. A ritual for organization.
4. A ritual to dispel bad habits or traits holding one back from their full potential.

Or do what you want. You're a magician — create!

Week 38 - Halphas - Rest/Reflect/Plan/Meditate

What did Halphas teach you this week? How is your

working relationship with Halphas? Did your energy vibe with his? How did it make you feel? Write down all the sensations, emotions, smells, sights, feelings, and thoughts that come to mind when you reflect on the past week's work. What lessons can you take from this week moving forward?

Even if you don't write all of this down, at least sit and reflect on it. Life is a constant learning process. If any of us stops learning, it probably means we're dead, or not long for this mortal coil.

WEEK 39: MALPHAS

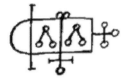

PRESIDENT
Color: Orange
Incense: Storax
Metal: Mercury
Planet: Mercury
Element: Air
Enn: Lirach tasa Malphas ayer
Date: April 11 - 20

Original Purpose: He can build houses and towers and will keep you informed of your enemy's every move. He gives good familiars. Allegedly if you give him a sacrifice he will immediately deceive you. (This is crap, btw.)

Author's Notes: He can help you build a foundation of safety at home and in the astral temple. Some invoke Malphas as a ward against psychic and physical assaults.

Week 39 - Malphas - Meditation

Today, while drawing Malphas' seal, I want you to not focus on how it looks (as some people are obsessed with aesthetics and will beat themselves up for crooked lines or imperfect scaling) but the areas Malphas rules over. I've always considered Malphas a big player when it comes to a person's core strength. Your inner Malphas is the source of your foundation. For some, that foundation is crumbling and cracking and needs some work, but for others, it's a strong foundation in confidence and self-reliance and has the ability to draw the help you need and foresee what is to come. Hence, Malphas is great to work with if you need the secure your foundation, start a rebuild, attract the help you need to make that happen, find inner confidence, and/or foresee what's coming to make sure your domain is well fortified.

That said, this won't apply to some of you since some of you already have stable foundations. You have a solid place to live, a career that helps you afford your needs (and perhaps your wants, too), you have familiars and friends and family. You have confidence and you feel secure in all of this - and your divination for what to come is fruitful. That is the overall foundation.

You can, however, apply this model to smaller parts of your life where you may not feel your foundation is as stable. For example - in your spiritual/magickal life, doing this course is helping you to further build a strong foundation from which to work on your Great Work. But it can be applied to other areas of learning, relationships, career matters, parenting, grandparenting, and even hobbies. Meditate on that today.

Also know that you can work with Malphas (and all Daemons for that matter) for one-off help. Like if you feel attacked, invoke Malphas in all four corners of your home or property and as for his protection and the safety of all who dwell there. Invoke him for wisdom when you find a crack in one of your foundations (metaphorically speaking), like when you discover that maybe your career isn't as stable as you thought it was. He can give good counsel on which direction to take. If you're looking for new familiars - there are numerous Daemons who can help with that (especially in the Goetia), but Malphas particularly brings you protective servitors and ones that will help you get shit done in your domain. Work with him during divination to give your session some extra oomph, or just carry his seal for that extra bit of confidence during your day.

Week 39 - Malphas - Freewrite

Today's freewriting exercise is simple (theoretically). I want you to examine your life currently, the foundation it's built on, and give it a thorough once over. Are you making enough money? Is your career where you want it to be? Are there things you need to do around your house? Is it time for you to bite the bullet and buy that property in the middle of nowhere? Is it time to quit your day job and start your own business? Is it time to start socking away more money for retirement, or investing more heavily in family and friends? What things can you do to help build a stronger foundation for your life? This is actually a meditation we should all do on a yearly basis. Assess where we are. Assess where we want to be. Examine whether or not we are content and sometimes happy, since happiness is not a state of being 100% of the time. Happiness comes in moments. Contentment, however, can be a state of being. If you're not content, what needs to change in order for you to be pleased with everything? A lot of times, when we're younger, it's all about the cash, and while income is good at helping us with contentment and more happy moments, we often discover, as we get older, it's people, relationships, and simpler things that bring contentment and more happy moments.

Week 39 - Malphas - Dreamwork

For tonight's dreamwork, go into sleep with the intent to speak to the Daemon and gain insight or wisdom. Don't even go in with any questions. Just the intent to speak with the Daemon. I know that seems counterintuitive since focusing on specifics often gleans more specific results, but sometimes leaving things a bit open ended and being open-minded about the outcome brings up things we didn't know about, or hadn't considered. You can do this with any Daemonic force, not just Malphas.

As always, keep your dream journal next to your bed so you can jot down whatever you remember from your dreams as soon as you wake up. You're also allowed to do what you want because you're an adult and all that. Remember that each day's post is merely a suggestion meant to motivate you to do the work and get to know the Goetic spirit we're exploring for the week.

Week 39 - Malphas - Invocation/Evocation #1

Today's suggested exercise in Invocation / Evocation is going to be brief and will give you an example of how not all "summonings", if you will, need to be elaborate rituals. I want you to take a premade Malphas pendant, or coin, or his seal that you've created out of paper, clay, or whatnot - and use Malphas's enn to draw the Daemonic force into the space around you. Once you feel the energy in the space change, ask Malphas to infuse the seal with the power of confidence. Hold the seal between your hands, visualizing confident and powerful vibrations filling it with a brilliant orange light. Do this for at least ten minutes. Next, make a note of this ritual in your journal and leave some space. For the next three days I want you to carry this seal with you and each night, note its effect on the people around you and more importantly, how carrying the seal affected your confidence.

Week 39 - Malphas - Invocation/Evocation #2

Today, invoke Malphas into your temple and do a divination session using the divination tool of your choice (as Malphas works well with most tools, especially scrying in crystals). Did you find you got more direct answers? More archaic answers? Hesitancy? A sense of eagerness? Were your visions clearer? Foggier? Your intuition sharp or cloudy? Different Daemons affect each magician differently. Record this experiment and your results in your journal.

Week 39 - Malphas - Create a Spell or Ritual

Today, create a spell/ritual/or magickal artifact for any of the following:

1. Confidence
2. To draw familiars
3. A divination device, or consecration of a divination device
4. Protection

Week 39 - Malphas - Rest/Reflect/Plan/Meditate

How did your week with Malphas go? Write any

insights or reflections about the work in your journal. And the bottom line - is Malphas a Daemon you'll work with again? Working with each Daemon, you'll notice some draw you more than others. That you feel more "at home" or a natural "click" with some, and not with others. On a Scale of 1-10, with 1 being NOT AT ALL, and 10 being THIS DAEMON IS MY NEW BFF, where did Malphas fall?

WEEK 40: RAUM

EARL
Color: Red
Incense: Dragon's Blood
Metal: Copper or Silver
Planet: Mars
Element: Air (Fire)
Enn: Furca na alle laris Raum
Date: April 21 – 30

Original Purpose: Steals treasure from kings. Destroys cities and dignities. Causes love between friends and foes. Tells all things past, present, and future.

Author's Notes: Invoke Raum to take down a mighty foe or adversary. Raum is also helpful in legal battles against large conglomerates. Seek Raum's wisdom to find personal strength when the odds are against you.

Week 40 – Raum – Meditation

So, the really great thing about Raum is he reminds me of Leviathan, except a Fire counterpart when it comes to the Justice/Wisdom factors. Today when you're drawing the seal and meditating on Raum, I want you to consider the purposes you might work with him when it comes to the Justice aspect of Vengeance. The confidence that wisdom brings, and the great power and responsibility of knowledge. You might also consider that Raum can reconcile friendships as well. Working with him to repair relationships is also on the table this week.

Week 40 - Raum - Freewrite

Today I want you to explore your temperament and any anger you might be holding onto in your life. You might be asking yourself, "What the hell?" But hear me out. Sometimes cursing is a knee jerk reaction, especially when we have no other recourse to deal with anger that won't result in possible jail time. Raum is good in helping people deal with their anger from hurt feelings or from being wronged. Explore this and keep it in mind for the rest of the week. You're also welcome to write about friendships, or things you want to learn, or new experiences you want to have. Think of these freewrites as a mind-dump exercise. A lot of people come back to me after doing freewriting telling me they seem to get more done on their freewriting days because they're able to get all the stuff on their mind out onto the page so they can focus on other things throughout their day.

How has the weekly freewriting exercise affected

you? That's possibly something you could freewrite about.

Week 40 - Raum - Dreamwork

For tonight's dreamwork, I want you to visualize the sigil and hear the enn of the Daemon in your mind as you're falling asleep. You might keep a copy of the seal under your mattress, but also keep it in a place you can see it while you're falling asleep. Or just give it a long hard look. Again, this week I want you to go into sleep without any expectations except to get a message from Raum. Nothing else. Keep your mind wide open.

The moment you wake up, write down anything you remember. Also, note how you slept. That's really important with any dreamwork exercise. Sometimes the answer is in the quality of your sleep, how refreshed you feel when you wake up, or how peaceful you feel.

Week 40 - Raum - Invocation/Evocation #1

Now, I'm not going to tell you how to construct your ritual space or perform your invocations/evocations here. Most magicians have their personal preferred method and whether it's a quick spell or an elaborate ritual is up to you when you do these invocations/evocations. Today, once you contact Raum via the enn (or an invocation of your own design — this is perfectly fine) and you feel the energy in the room change, I want you to burn a request to Raum (sealed with a drop of your blood if you aren't afraid to do blood magick) to repair or strengthen your relationship(s), or the relationships of people you know and care about. Then, through the coming week, watch those relationships for signs of change and note any significant incidents.

Week 40 - Raum- Invocation/Evocation #2

Today, I want you to invoke Raum, then sit comfortably in your ritual space and draw that Daemonic energy into you with the intent of feeling more confident in your own wisdom or your own knowledge. Once you feel strong, close the ritual thanking Raum for his presence and Daemonic force, and then go about your day. Tomorrow, reflect on how you felt in the 24 hours directly after this ritual. What changed? What didn't change? Were you comfortable with this exercise? Why or why not?

Remember that journaling our magickal experiments may seem like an annoying time suck, but in 10 years, you may find yourself thrilled to go back and read these journals because they will show you just how much you've grown and changed. Reflecting on our experiences on paper also helps us to make more sense of our experiences, and to draw more well-thought conclusions.

Week 40 - Raum - Create a Spell or Ritual

Today, create a spell/ritual/or magickal artifact working with Raum for one of the following:

1. For Justice
2. For knowledge/wisdom
3. To Reconcile a Relationship

Week 40 - Raum - Rest/Reflect/Plan/Meditate

What did your week with Raum reveal to you? How was the working relationship? Have you considered going back through your journal and rating your working relationship on that 1-10 scale (or your own rating system) with all the Goetia spirits you've worked with so far? Take at least ten minutes every Sunday to reflect on the previous week's work. Do it over your morning coffee/tea/beverage of choice. Incorporating the spiritual into everyday life, by the time this course is over and if you're doing something (no matter how small) every day, will become the norm.

WEEK 41: FOCALOR

DUKE
Color: Green
Incense: Sandalwood
Metal: Copper
Planet: Venus
Element: Water
Enn: En Jedan on ca Focalor
Date: May 1 - 10

Original Purpose: He will slay the magician's enemies and protect the magician if the magician commands it.

Author's Notes: Invoke for execration magicks and situations you wish to resolve quickly and in your favor. If you dream of Focalor or his sigil, it is a warning that someone wishes you ill and may be planning your downfall.

I am going to be honest here and share with you that Focalor is, by far, one of my favorite Goetic Spirits. If you can develop a strong working relationship with him, he gives good advice, will give you the heads up when shit goes down so you're not left with your ass hanging out, and can help you pick yourself up after a major setback (but not in a coddling way - more like a pragmatic motivational way). There is a direct connection between Focalor and Lucifuge Rofocal. As Focalor is an anagram of Rofocal.

Whether they're the same divine intelligence is debatable as each magician will have their own opinion on that, but there is definitely a link and a similarity in energy. One could be an avatar of the other, or perhaps they're the same, just different degrees of the same. It's food for thought anyway.

Week 41 - Focalor - Meditation

While Focalor is one of the ultimate Daemonic forces for execration magick and destroying obstacles, many traditional Daemonolaters who work with the Goetic spirits tend to view Focalor as a protectorate, or a Daemonic force you go to for wise counsel, not only with regard to disputes, but also with regard to emotional analysis. That's an aspect of Focalor a lot of people miss. He can help you learn to analyze and deal with emotional upset, fear, anger, and even how we react when attacked or provoked. So, while you're drawing his seal today, I want you to consider all of this and make a mental note on anything that comes up in your meditation or stands out.

Week 41 - Focalor - Freewrite

Today, I want you to write about anything that came up in yesterday's meditation that stood out or came up unexpectedly. I also want you to consider your feelings about Focalor as a protectorate, as well as a Daemonic force one might seek out for sage advice on matters involving emotional responses that feel bad and the self-analysis involved in observing our emotions before acting on them. Are there any situations you can think of where you wished you'd paused and reflected on what you were feeling and why you felt that way before acting on that emotion? Or are you naturally one of those people who reflects first, then reacts? In what ways would it benefit you to control your emotions instead of letting them control you? Or vice versa? What are the drawbacks of controlling your emotions?

Week 41 - Focalor - Dreamwork

Tonight, I want you to specifically go into sleep with the intention of receiving a symbol that Focalor can give you (that you both will agree upon) as an advance warning to something threatening coming your way. Immediately upon waking up, write down what the dream revealed. Don't be disappointed if you got nothing. You can, technically, try this dreamwork exercise every night this week. The Dreamwork is one of the easier exercises to do nightly without expending much time or effort, and I hope most of you are doing it. The only time I would recommend holding off on dreamwork is if you're not getting enough sleep and you need your rest. Because oftentimes dreamwork can turn into lucid/controlled dream walking, which can sometimes exacerbate exhaustion and lack of quality sleep.

Week 41 - Focalor - Invocation/Evocation #1

You will need the following for today's exercise if you choose to do this:

• 1 Vial of Olive Oil blessed in the name of Focalor.
• Sigils of Focalor for every room in your home. If your home has 4 rooms, you need four. If you have 50 rooms, you need 50. If you have your own property, you will need four additional seals and a garden trowel.

Go into each room of your home one by one and do the following:

1. Invoke Focalor using the enn or your own personal invocation (do this in EVERY room).
2. Ask him to protect your home.
3. Dab one of the sigils with the blessed olive oil and

place it somewhere in the room.

4. Anoint the top of each door frame and window frame in the room with the blessed olive oil saying, "Focalor, may your protection of this space and all who dwell within it be strong."

5. Repeat until all rooms have been anointed and the sigil placed.

If you have property, go to each of the four corners of the property one by one and do the following at every corner.

1. Invoke Focalor using the enn or your own personal invocation.

2. Ask him to protect your property.

3. Dab the sigil with the blessed olive oil.

4. Dig a hole.

5. Place the sigil in the hole and bury it.

6. Repeat until the final four sigils have been buried.

7. Pour the remainder of the olive oil near the threshold of your home. You can even pour some at the front door and some at the back. Additionally, you can skip this part and keep any leftover oil for other work with Focalor.

You will NOT thank the Daemon and ask it to leave. You will allow your space to permeate in Daemonic energy.

Tomorrow, I want you to jot down in your journal

how the protection on your home makes your space feel. Because oftentimes protections like this will change the feeling of a space.

Also know that you can do this ritual any time with any Daemonic force you choose, and you can also do this astrally if you cannot do it physically, but I've found the physicality of the ritual more satisfying.

Week 41 - Focalor - Invocation/Evocation #2

Today for your Invocation, I want you to do a scrying or ascension session to speak with Focalor, asking for general wisdom, for advice on any persistent fears, anger, or sadness, or anything else along those lines.
What came of this session? Did you find Focalor easy to connect with? Distant? If you didn't get anything, don't feel defeated. Sometimes learning to scry or speak with Daemons can take time and lots of practice.

Week 41 - Focalor - Create a Spell or Ritual

Create a Spell, Ritual, or Magickal Artifact in the name of Focalor for one of the following:

1. To crush enemies or obstacles.
2. For protection.
3. To warn against danger.

4. For gaining sage advice

Week 41 - Focalor - Rest/Reflect/Plan/Meditate

Did you have a connection with Focalor? Does he feel right in the role of a protectorate for you? It's okay if the answer is no. Not everyone will feel this connection. Did you receive any advice from him that you will be able to utilize right away? Did you have any revelations about yourself? Finally — is working with the Goetic Spirits bringing up the shadow work/self-work you need to do in order to live a more authentic life in accordance with your Great Work? Do you see any common themes emerging as you're doing the work?

WEEK42: VEPAR

DUKE
Color: Green
Incense: Sandalwood
Metal: Copper
Planet: Venus
Element: Water
Enn: On ca Vepar Ag Na
Date: May 11 -20

Original Purpose: A Daemon of Water who can control ships and the waters (and storms). She can also cause men to die in three days by putrefying wounds or sores.

Author's Notes: Vepar is an excellent Daemon to invoke if you want to explore your emotions or behaviors prior to making a change. Good for cursing toxic emotions as well.

Week 42 - Vepar - Meditation

As you're drawing Vepar's seal, I want you to pay close attention to your emotional state. I want you to observe your emotions and really take note of them. What kinds of emotions does the seal evoke in you? What does the name Vepar "feel" like? Vepar is all about feelings and emotions, including emotional control and behaviors stemming from emotions.

This is why Vepar is a solid spirit to work with when it comes to execration magick (as well as cursing our own toxic emotional states), dealing with emotional compromise and upset, increasing our emotional intelligence, and making behavioral changes to deal with toxic habits or even negative self-talk. So, consider all of this as we move through the week.

Please keep in mind that Vepar is also great for healing magick, especially wounds and breaks that need healing. That which can cause illness can also cure in the realm of Divine Intelligence. It's just a matter of where you take it.

Week 42 - Vepar - Freewrite

Today I want you to evoke, in your mind, the memory of a situation that makes you feel emotionally vulnerable, or angry, or deeply troubled. Now, observe the emotion - detach yourself from it. Write about the situation. Why does this memory bring up these emotions? How does it feel to observe rather than react? Now remind yourself that YOU have complete control of your emotional state and can banish anger, sadness, jealousy etc.... just by changing your perception. How does this concept of control make you feel? Do you feel that you can control your reactions and emotional states to this degree? Why or why not? Do you believe you can choose to be a victim or choose to be miserable? Just go with this line of thinking and see where it takes you.

Week 42 - Vepar- Dreamwork

Tonight, I want you to take any toxic feelings you have toward someone else, or a situation, and bring them into your dreams with you. If you can take control of the dream and do some dream walking, take those feelings and lay them out in your astral or dream temple. Then call on Vepar to help you deal with the toxicity that could be holding you back.
What comes of this exercise? Remember, it's okay if you don't get a result. And sometimes you'll get a result just by confronting something that has been weighing on you.

Week 42 - Vepar - Invocation/Evocation #1

Every invocation must have a purpose. A central goal behind it. Today, do an invocation (that works with your magickal paradigm or practice) and choose one of the following purposes to focus on:

-Healing Emotional or Physical (yourself or someone else)
-Destroying/Cursing Something or Someone Toxic
-Personal Transformation
-Taking Your Power Back From Someone Else

Week 42 - Vepar - Invocation/Evocation #2

Today, I'd like those of you who practice grimoiric magick to do a standard Goetic ritual with Vepar to speak with the spirit in the mirror. For the rest of you, perform your invocation in accordance with your personally preferred method and then do a divination session using the divination device of your choice. See what insights Vepar has for you. Go into this open-minded if you want to be surprised, or with something specific. It's up to you.

Week 42 - Vepar - Create a Spell or Ritual

In previous iterations of this class, I always called the "Create a Spell or Ritual" day of the class, Daemonic Arts and Crafts because I had students devise some type of magickal artifact that they could keep from their work with the Daemon and use for future work. Some folks chose to create sigil sets. Others would create talismans. Others still would paint or draw or compose a piece of music or writing. So today, that's what I want you to do.

Create something tangible that's a spell or ritual for Vepar in and of itself. Listen to your intuition and let Vepar inspire you.

Week 42 - Vepar - Rest/Reflect/Plan/Meditate

What did you discover during your work with Vepar this week? Maybe some pent-up issues you hadn't dealt with? Or perhaps you learned that you've successfully booted all the toxicity from your life. Be sure to write all this down. I know all the writing can get tedious, but if you don't have time, consider trying a dictation app on your phone! That way you only have to speak your feelings and thoughts about your magickal work, print it out, and put it into a three-ring binder. Or keep it on your computer in a word processor file. There are plenty of ways to keep a record of your personal journey.

WEEK 43: SABNOCK

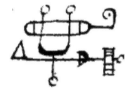

MARQUIS
Color: Violet
Incense: Jasmine
Metal: Silver
Planet: Moon
Element: Fire
Enn: Tasa Sabnock on ca Lirach
Date: May 21 - 31

Original Purpose: Builds high towers, cities, and castles and protects them. He can also make people sick with festering sores.

Author's Notes: Invoke Sabnock as a protection ward in your home or astral temple and anyone who attacks your spaces protected by him will become ill immediately. Once they call off their attack, the illness will subside. It seems to be a strong deterrent.

Week 43 - Sabnock - Meditation

Sabnock is glorious! This spirit has such an amazing Fiery-Watery energy going on that you can't help but be inspired and find the energy to get things done. Even if that thing is diving deep into some deep emotional work. There's also a creative aspect to Sabnock that is often overlooked by those who limit themselves to whatever descriptions we writers put in our books. But Sabnock is also, traditionally, a great protectorate for the home and workplace. And yes - Sabnock will help you destroy your enemies, or at least the rent-free space they're taking up in your thoughts. So as you're meditating on Sabnock today, and perhaps drawing out his seal, keep all of this in mind, or just focus on your breath and the sigil, keep an open mind, and jot down notes on anything that comes to you. Don't let my interpretation of a Daemon, or anyone else's, limit you thinking or your experience.

Week 43 - Sabnock - Freewrite

Today's writing prompts for your freewrite can start as, "I need protection from..." to "I need to destroy..." or you can start with "I feel" statements. Or maybe you just feel inspired to write a story about a person who goes for a walk in the woods and finds a sigil talisman hanging from a branch. Before you start writing, take a few minutes to center yourself, and ask Sabnock to be present. What does he inspire? Perhaps your freewriting session will turn into an automatic writing/drawing session. One never knows.

Week 43 - Sabnock- Dreamwork

Again, slip into sleep tonight with the intention to speak with Sabnock, and perhaps he'll share wisdom, inspiration, or messages to help you solve an issue.

Week 43 - Sabnock - Invocation/Evocation #1

Today, invoke Sabnock and in his name, charge an item in your home for protection against physical and psychic harm. Keep the item in your home and your home will always be a safe space. Recharge the item monthly with the intention of protection and the energy of Sabnock. (You're also welcome to do a request ritual, a scrying session, or an ascension session.)

Week 43 - Sabnock - Invocation/Evocation #2

Today, choose one of the following to work with Sabnock:

1. Draw Sabnock into you before working on a creative project.
2. Ask Sabnock to destroy negative feelings/thoughts. (Or self-sabotaging thoughts)
3. Invoke Sabnock - write a to-do list - and ask

Sabnock for the energy to complete it.

Week 43 - Sabnock - Create a Spell or Ritual

Today, I want you to create a ritual, spell, or talisman for inspiration with the aid of Sabnock.

Week 43 - Sabnock - Rest/Reflect/Plan/Meditate

How was your week with Sabnock? Do you feel emotionally refreshed? I find him emotionally refreshing. Working with him is like having a cathartic cleanse sometimes. Be sure to write your reflection from the week in your journal.

WEEK 44: SHAX

MARQUIS
Color: Violet
Incense: Jasmine
Metal: Silver
Planet: Moon
Element: Air
Enn: Ayer Avage Shax aken
Date: June 1 - 10

Original Purpose: Steal money from kings, fetch horses for the magician, he sometimes gives good familiars, and he can take away a person's sight, hearing, and understanding.

Author's Notes: Shax is a gift giver. By gifts I don't mean material items but rather after working with him the magician might find a way to obtain something he wants. Or someone beneficial will come into his/her life. Sometimes Shax will temporarily take something from you only to give it back once you've learned to appreciate it.

Week 44 - Shax - Meditation

Because Shax brings opportunity as is the giver of gifts, ask yourself what opportunities you need right now as you draw the sigil. Pay attention to any thoughts or images that cross your mind as you're doing this. Set your intention to discover new opportunities this week.

Week 44 - Shax - Freewrite

I am going to ask you to do a weird exercise today. I want you to start jotting down ideas for gifts to give family and friends for the Solstice season. Whether you practice a secular Christmas with family, a quiet solstice, or a two week long Yuletide, planning is key. And since Shax is the gift giver, it stands to reason he's got some great ideas for gifts. If you were Shax, what gifts would you give people? More common sense? Help? Their favorite dinner? A day of relaxation? Asking yourself questions like this will not only generate great gift ideas, but also ask yourself what gifts you could really use right now. Write them down even if they feel unrealistic. A million dollars is perfectly acceptable to write about. What would you do if you received the gift you wanted? How would it change your life? Would it make things easier? More challenging? More exciting? How could you help change the lives of others through giving a gift? What does this line of thinking inspire in you?

Week 44 - Shax Dreamwork

Try going into dreamwork tonight with the intent of seeking a familiar from Shax. What happens? Did you wake up with your pet staring at you? Did you dream of your familiar? Does the house feel differently the morning after? Do you feel different?

Week 44 - Shax - Invocation/Evocation #1

For today's invocation, I suggest invoking the Daemon into the space and then doing a scrying session with the intent of gaining answers to questions, or discovering wisdom.

Week 44 - Shax - Invocation/Evocation #2

Today, use your invocation for one of the following purposes:

1. Taking someone else's focus off of you.
2. Re-learning to appreciate things you may be taking for granted. An appreciation ritual, where you focus on all the things you're grateful for, may be just the thing you need to realize just how good you have things. Especially if you're prone to concentrate on the negatives in life.
Week 44 - Shax - Create a Spell or Ritual

Create a spell or ritual for one of the following:
1. To obtain a familiar from Shax.

2. To gain understanding.
3. To remove a curse.
4. To become invisible to someone else.

Week 44 - Shax - Rest/Reflect/Plan/Meditate

What did this week, and Shax, teach you about yourself? Did any deep shadow work/pathworking come up that surprised you? How did your energy mesh with Shax's? Is Shax a Daemonic force you'd work with again?

WEEK 45: VINE

KING
Color: Yellow
Incense: Frankincense
Metal: Gold
Planet: Sun
Element: Water
Enn: Eyesta nas Vine ca laris
Date: June 11 -20

Original Purpose: Sometimes listed as an Earl. He can build towers, destroy walls and conjure great storms. He is also about discovering hidden things including much about magick.

Author's Notes: Vine is a magician's Daemon. Invoke him when you want to learn more about magick or you wish to better understand something you're studying (with regard to magick).

Week 45 - Vine - Meditation

This week we're going to take a deep look into your magickal practice, what skills you wish to learn more about, what areas of magick you wish to become more skilled in, and how to give your magick some extra oomph with the help of Vine. Think of Vine as a magical teacher of sorts. This also means that he appreciates magicians who create — the whole purpose of the magician to begin with. Whatever you create makes a good offering. What are you creating? What is your magic? Ask yourself these questions while you draw the sigil and meditate on the virtues of Vine.

Week 45 - Vine- Freewrite

Today, I want you to write up what you hope to learn this week based on what your meditation yielded yesterday. I was recently asked if you could combine the meditation and freewrite in one day directly afterward, and the answer is yes. You can also do dreamwork on the same day as something else if you need to combine your work to fit around your schedule. Write down whatever you are inspired to write about Vine, your magickal practice (or lack thereof), your magickal skills, and WHAT YOU CREATE! What are you creating for yourself? A life with a solid, quality foundation for personal success and satisfaction? Or are you simply creating havoc and drama? Does what you create help you to mind your own business and fulfill your great work?

Week 45 - Vine- Dreamwork

Tonight, I want you to focus on Vine's seal as you fall asleep and try to take control of any dreams and head to your astral temple for some magickal work. What does this experiment produce if anything? Does focusing on the Daemon's sigil, and even saying his enn aloud (or in your head) before sleep produce any results? How was your quality of sleep?

Week 45 - Vine - Invocation/Evocation #1

Today, I want you to do an invocation, vibrating the enn until the energy in the room changes, specifically to draw the energy of Vine into the temple, perhaps even into yourself, just so you can blend and combine your energy with the Daemon's. If you feel uncomfortable with this, you can do an invocation/evocation of choice and do your own work. If you don't feel uncomfortable - draw the energy in and carry it with you for the next 24 hours. How did Vine's energy make you feel? Were you more alert? More present? Anxious? Exhausted? What changed in your personal demeanor due to trying this?

Week 45 - Vine- Invocation/Evocation #2

Today you're welcome to do a traditional scrying session with Vine, or a simple request ritual, or a ritual of your choosing. Remember that Vine can help you build magickal skills as well, so you can invoke him before practicing a certain skill and asking him to guide you to improvement.

Week 45 - Vine - Create a Spell or Ritual

Since the function of the magician is to be a creator - today I want you to create a magickal artifact to honor Vine and your own magickal practice. It can be as simple as you charging an talisman with Vine's energy, or creating a talisman you can pull out any time you want to amp up the power in your rituals. Be sure to keep detailed notes on what you created, as well as leaving space to make notes on how well the item works when utilized.

Week 45 - Vine - Rest/Reflect/Plan/Meditate

What was your biggest takeaway from Vine this week? Did you find areas you could use improvement? Did you discover something about your skills that helped you get to the next level? What did you learn about your creation process and what you create?

WEEK 46: BIFRONS

EARL
Color: Red
Incense: Dragon's Blood
Metal: Copper or Silver
Planet: Mars
Element: Earth
Enn: Avage secore Bifrons remie tasa
Date: June 21 – July 1

Original Purpose: Lights candles on the graves of the dead and can invoke the dead. He can make a man knowledgeable in astronomy and other sciences. He can teach the properties of stones and woods.

Author's Notes: Another Necromancy Daemon. Work with Bifrons to communicate with the dead. This would be the Daemon invoked for a funeral ceremony to help usher the dead on their journey. Also invoke during rituals to honor ancestors or to learn to accept death.

Week 46- Bifrons - Meditation

While I'm sure you may be tired of Necromancy, depending on how much work you did as the veil thinned this year, this week with Bifrons can be utilized to continue Necromantic work as well as learning to accept death and change. Perhaps there's a big change coming up in your life. New baby. Retirement. New job. Big move. Divorce. Marriage. Death of someone close to you or a pet. You can use this week to work on any of this as your needs dictate. If you find there is nothing in these areas you can work on, you're welcome to simply meditate and allow the Daemon to bring ideas and inspiration to you. Think about all of this as you draw the seal of Bifrons, contemplating every curve, every intricate detail of the sigil.

Week 46- Bifrons- Freewrite

Today in your journal I'd like you to write about how you deal with change, loss, and grief. We grieve a lot of changes in our lives like the ones I brought up in yesterday's meditation. Never gloss over your own emotional reactions to changes (and not just death). Write about whatever comes up during your journaling and consider what you can do to help yourself weather loss better.

Week 46- Bifrons- Dreamwork

Tonight, as you fall asleep, I want you to set your intent on Bifrons escorting you to the grave of a loved one or bringing them forward so you can speak to them in a dream. Did anything come of this? Did you see your dead loved one? Did you acquire wisdom from the Daemon? Did you sleep heavily or lightly? Was the sleep restful or restless? Write all of this in your dream/sleep journal.

Week 46- Bifrons - Invocation/Evocation #1

Today, since we're still within a good period to work Necromancy, I'd like you to invoke Bifrons and ask him to bring forward a loved one from the other side. It could be a grandparent you didn't know, too. Then I want you to either do a scrying session or just LISTEN and see what you hear. Ask any questions you might have. Necromancy doesn't need to be formal and complicated. If you knew this person in life, did you feel their presence? Did you see them or hear them?

Often, people will report that this type of work with Bifrons can be eye opening or even jolting depending on the person. Write down your experience.

You are welcome to do your own thing here. You are welcome to just do another meditation, just this time, after invocation/evocation.

Week 46- Bifrons - Invocation/Evocation #2

Today let's do something a little different. I want you to take a walk to somewhere in nature near your home. It might be a bit chilly so bundle up. If you can walk to a graveyard, do that. Do it during the day - it doesn't have to be dark out. Find a place in nature (or the graveyard) to sit in contemplation and invoke/evoke the Daemon using the enn either in your head, or beneath your breath (as to not draw attention from passersby). Now I want you to just sit quietly with the energy, focusing on your breath and feeling the Daemonic energy out. A lot of people find this type of invocation meditation useful when they're faced with abrupt life changes and acceptance of change. Do you feel soothed by this exercise? Unsettled? Some people find Bifrons a bit strong and altering energy wise. Be sure to make detailed notes of how his energy makes you feel.

If for some reason you don't have time to wander around in a park or graveyard, you're welcome to go out onto a balcony, porch, or backyard, too.

Week 46- Bifrons- Create a Spell or Ritual

Today, create a spell or ritual for one of the following:

1. To bless/create a scrying mirror in the name of

Bifrons that you'll use in necromancy.

2. A ritual with Bifrons to weather change.

3. A ritual that honors your ancestors. Think about what your ancestors would be proud of and use that as a guideline here.

Week 46- Bifrons - Rest/Reflect/Plan/Meditate

Today, write up your concluding thoughts on Bifrons and catch up on writing everything up in your journal. How did your week go? Did you feel close to your dearly departed dead? Did you feel you weathered change well this week? How do YOU feel? Write all of this down.

WEEK 47: UVALL/VUAL

DUKE
Color: Green
Incense: Sandalwood
Metal: Copper
Planet: Venus
Element: Water
Enn: (also Uvall or Voval)– As ana nany on ca Uvall/Vual.
Date: July 2 -11

Original Purpose: A Daemon of friendship and love.

Author's Notes: Wearing the sigil of Uvall when going to a party or social gathering will draw people to you.

TRY THIS EXERCISE THIS WEEK: Carry his seal any time you go to a social gathering to draw people (and potential new friends/associates) to you.

Week 47 - Vual - Meditation

Today, as you draw the seal and contemplate Vual, I want you to take a few minutes to think about your emotional state regarding your relationships. You may even jot down a few notes about this afterward.

Week 47 -Vual - Freewrite

Some things to ask yourself during today's freewrite exercise: When you think of love, what emotions come up? When you think of friendship, what emotions do you have? What and where are your thoughts drawn to? In which way could the emotional aspects of your relationships be improved upon? Write about anything these questions inspire.

Week 47 - Vual - Dreamwork

Before you go to sleep tonight, I want you to formulate 1-4 questions about a friendship/relationship you'd like answers to. Place Vual's seal beneath your pillow or mattress. Focus on the Daemon as you fall asleep and your intention to have your questions answered. Immediately upon waking, write down anything from your dreams that you remember.

Week 47 - Vual - Invocation/Evocation #1

Invoke the Daemon and scry for the answers to any of your relationship questions. You can also do an ascension session if this is easier for you.

Week 47 - Vual - Invocation/Evocation #2

Today after invoking/evoking Vual, perform a simple request ritual to Vual where you write down what it is you're seeking and burn it in the offering bowl - asking the Daemon for wisdom about any relationship issues (this can include romantic, friendship, or familial relationships) you might be having, or asking for a resolution to a relationship issue. Leave space in your journal to record any manifestations from this ritual. Remember that manifestation may not just be a result in the relationship itself, but also in your perception or understanding of the relationship. Sometimes we just need to shift our perception in order to solve an "issue."

Week 47 - Vual - Create a Spell or Ritual

Today, you can create a spell, ritual, or magickal artifact (i.e., a talisman or whatnot) with Vual for:

1. Reconciling fractured friendships.
2. Drawing new friendships.
3. Insight into your relationships with others.

Week 47 - Vual - Rest/Reflect/Plan/Meditate

What did this week's work with Vual teach you?
Maybe he taught you that your relationships are
solid (Daemons can teach us that everything is okay
sometimes). Or maybe that work was needed, or
that another relationship may not be worth
salvaging. Hopefully, the exercises this week also
taught you who you are thankful/grateful to have in
your life. It's also an excellent exercise to sit down
every now and again and think of all the ways we're
blessed. Especially when we're feeling like nothing
is going right.

WEEK 48: HAAGENTI

PRESIDENT
Color: Orange
Incense: Storax
Metal: Mercury
Planet: Mercury
Element: Earth (Water)
Enn: Haagenti on ca Lirach
Date: July 12 - 21

Original Purpose: Makes men wise, turns water to wine, all metals to gold etc.

Author's Notes: A Daemon of alchemical transformation. Can take something ordinary or negative and help you change it into something extraordinary. For example, if life gives you lemons, make lemonade.

Week 48 - Haagenti- Meditation

Today as you draw the sigil, I want you to imagine what can be. Yes, this is an open-ended statement if there ever was one, but it needs to be so you can find what needs adjustment. What can be? Which metaphoric water would you like to turn into metaphoric wine?

Week 48 - Haagenti - Freewrite

Today we're going to explore the idea of transformation, changing situations or things about ourselves. Is there a bad habit you'd like to replace with something better? Like instead of sitting in front of the TV, maybe you want to add some yoga and 500 words of that novel you keep telling everyone you're going to write — someday. Well, today's the day to start thinking about all these transformations and changes we want to make (whether it's deep cleaning the bathrooms or altering our appearance) and explore why we haven't done it, and what we can do to get the ball rolling.

Week 48 - Haagenti- Dreamwork

Tonight, I don't want you to focus on the Daemon at all. Just slip the sigil beneath your mattress, pillow, or bed, and go to sleep like you normally do. Make sure you make any notes about dreams or quality of sleep in your dream journal. Keeping a dream journal isn't just about dreams and gauging our mental health, but also the quality of our rest. The quality of our rest can affect our mental well-being, our physical energy - and hence our magick.

Week 48 - Haagenti - Invocation/Evocation #1

Today, invoke Haagenti, then visualize the Daemon's energy melding with your own. Pay close attention to any thoughts or feelings as you're doing this. You may even try some automatic writing/drawing. You're also welcome to simply do some deep breathing.

Week 48 - Haagenti - Invocation/Evocation #2

For the week's second evocation/invocation, I want you think about a transformation you'd like to make within yourself. Again, a bad habit, a negative thinking pattern, or even something physical about yourself (be realistic) and then burn a request to have Haagenti help you with your change. As the request burns, visualize yourself changed and a better situation manifested for you.

Leave space in your journal after rituals like this so you can make notes about what the ritual manifested at a later date.

Week 48 - Haagenti - Create a Spell or Ritual

Today, create a spell or ritual with the aid of Haagenti for:

1. Self-transformation of some sort
2. To alchemize your weaknesses to one of your

strengths.

3. To Change situations or manifest positive results.

Week 48 - Haagenti – Rest / Reflect / Plan / Meditate

What areas for self-reflection and self-work were highlighted this week? Write it down in your journal. While it's unlikely you'll have time to tackle all of this RIGHT NOW, it will give you ideas of where you need to go with your pathworking in the future. Also note any patterns you're noticing as you work your way through each Goetic spirit. Certain situations will continually crop up, especially if they're important for you now. Remember that you know what you need. You need to just trust in the process and the Daemonic to show you where things need adjustment and work.

WEEK 49: PROCEL/CROCELL

DUKE
Color: Green
Incense: Sandalwood
Metal: Copper
Planet: Venus
Element: Water
Enn (also Procel): Jedan tasa Crocell on ca
Date: July 22 – August 1

Original Purpose: Teaches liberal science and geometry. He can find water and warm it.

Author's Notes: Another Water Daemon. Invoke Crocell to soften aggressive or sharp emotions and warm the cold-hearted. Crocell can help people see the other side of an argument and not be so quick to judge.

Week 49 - Crocell- Meditation

This week is all about compassion and empathy for ourselves and for others. This week will hopefully offer perspective and help you gain more wisdom and cause you to judge less. So, as you're drawing the sigil today, I want you to become hyper-aware of the thoughts popping in and out of your head, and how many of them are judgmental. The thing is, we make hundreds of judgments a day without even realizing we do it. It's natural. But how many of those judgments are negative? What negative self-talk might be in there? Which judgments aren't useful/helpful?

Week 49 - Crocell- Freewrite

Whatever you meditated on yesterday — expound on that. Pick one thing that jumps out at you from yesterday's meditation and spend ten minutes writing. What comes up? You may find the issue is part of something larger, or that what you thought wasn't an issue is the real issue. Just follow your train of thought. Can you find healing in addressing an issue of compassion? Do you need more compassion for yourself? For others? Both?

Week 49 - Crocell- Dreamwork

Tonight, after putting the seal in the appropriate place (under bed, mattress, or pillow), I want you to go to bed having compassion for yourself and for others. I want you to think of something that made you angry or frustrated about yourself or someone else during your day and take a moment to find compassion for you or the other person. Try to fall asleep in that feeling of compassion. When you wake up - immediately write down how you feel upon waking up. Does ending your day with compassion warrant more experimentation?

Week 49 - Crocell- Invocation/Evocation #1

Tonight, I want you to invoke Crocell, draw the Daemon's energy into your own, and ask the Daemon to promote emotional healing, compassion and empathy in your life. Sit with this for 10-15 minutes, thank the Daemon, close your ritual space. Leave room in your journal for manifestations from this ritual.
As always, you're welcome to do a traditional Goetic working, or your own work based on what you want to work with the Daemon on.

Week 49 - Crocell - Invocation/Evocation #2

Today, I want you to try something a little different. While you're welcome to do whatever type of invocation/evocation that works for you, I'd like to suggest you invoke Crocell at some point during your day and ask to see through another person's eyes. Then shift your perspective and actually visualize yourself seeing through that person's eyes. It could be your boss, a co-worker, a friend or family member, or even a pet. You can do this in a matter of a few minutes no matter where you are. Some of you will have no results with this, others may experience strong effects with this. Be sure to make notes every time you try this.

For those of you with less time, I at least recommend carrying the seal of each Daemon we're working with for the week and taking some notes on whether or not anything manifested.

Week 49 - Crocell - Create a Spell or Ritual

Create a spell or ritual with Crocell for any of the following:

1. Healing (Emotional)
2. Wisdom in judgment.
3. Compassion, perspective, or empathy.
4. To help you adjust your consciousness to see a situation from another POV.

Week 49 - Crocell - Rest/Reflect/Plan/Meditate

What did Crocell teach you about your perspective and judgment? Have you experienced any emotional healing? Have you found negative feelings softened or changed? What other things did your work with Crocell reveal to you?

Only 27 more weeks to go. How are you doing? What are your biggest challenges keeping up with immersion? How are you managing those challenges? If all you can do is daily meditation and carrying the seal of the Daemon with you - do that!

But do try to write at least a paragraph each Sunday about how your previous week went, and any thoughts or reflections about the Daemonic force for that week. Even that will bring things to light, and you may find that even simple meditation is bringing about changes in your perspective and life overall.

WEEK 50: FURCAS

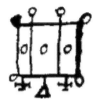

KNIGHT
Color: Black
Incense: Myrrh
Metal: Lead
Planet: Saturn
Element: Air
Enn: (also Furcus) Secore on ca Furcas remie
Date: August 2 -11

Original Purpose: Teaches pyromancy, astrology, chiromancy, logic and philosophy.

Author's Notes: Work with Furcas when learning to read natal charts, palms or learning clairvoyant skills (including all types of scrying, not just pyromancy). Note that Furcas takes his arte very seriously and expects those who seek him to do the same. If you are not serious, expect a stern "smack down".

Week 50 - Furcas - Meditation

Furcas is often worked with to help magicians hone skills in divination, including palm reading and fire scrying. He can also help us learn astrology and divination. So today, while drawing his seal, I want you to focus on what skills you'd like to work on this week. Maybe you'd like to have your natal chart done. Perhaps you'll want to pick up a book about scrying or cheiromancy and give it a read. That can be part of this week's work if you don't have time to do rituals or freewriting, or whatnot.

Week 50 - Furcas- Freewrite

For today's freewrite, I want you to draft a learning schedule you can implement at the beginning of the year to help you hone a magickal skill. It could be something as simple as spending half an hour a week doing some form of divination. Or it could be a goal like, I want to read 6 magick books this year. Or this year I'm going to work through Franz Bardon's *Initiation Into Hermetics*. Whatever it is - set these goals for 2023 now.

Week 50 - Furcas- Dreamwork

Tonight, rest your mind. Put the sigil beneath your pillow, bed, or mattress (or put it on a whiteboard on the wall or whatever), but just gaze at it and fall asleep with no intention for anything to happen.

When you wake up, make a note of how restful your sleep was. How do you feel mentally? Knowing how different Daemons and Daemonic energy (if you're invoking before bed) affects you during sleep can be a good tool in your arsenal. Because when you need that particular affect from your sleep again, you'll know which Daemon to work with for better rest, vivid dreams, or whatnot.

Week 50 - Furcas - Invocation/Evocation #1

Today, you're welcome to do a traditional or modified goetic ritual. Since the original goetic ritual is a scrying ritual so you can speak with the Daemonic force in the black mirror inside the triangle of art, I think it's always a good ritual to do for one of your Invocations/Evocations of Daemons who deal with scrying. Though Furcas does deal more with fire scrying. Instead of a mirror in the triangle of art, why not try a candle flame? Improvise. Experiment. You're a magician. Create.

Week 50 - Furcas- Invocation/Evocation #2

Take a sigil of Furcas and invoke the Daemon over it. Imbue all the energy of Furcas you can visualize into it. Now carry it with you over the weekend. What insights and lessons did you get from this exercise?

Week 50 - Furcas- Create a Spell or Ritual

Consider planetary correspondences when creating today's spell or ritual with Furcas for one of the following:

1. To learn a magickal art or to retain esoteric information.
2. To boost one's ability for spirit communication.
3. To boost one's fire scrying sessions or to see deeper into someone's palm.
4. To boost one's communication skills overall.

Week 50 - Furcas - Rest/Reflect/Plan/Meditate

Do you feel more confident in your scrying skills after your week with Furcas? Did you learn a new technique or something about your gift or process of divination? How was your communication with the spirit world? Did your astrology report help you to understand yourself more deeply, or a recent situation? Did you learn new information? Make a note of any of this if it applies, as well as your general impression of this particular Daemonic force.

WEEK 51: BALAM

KING
Color: Yellow
Incense: Frankincense
Metal: Gold
Planet: Sun
Element: Earth
Enn: Lirach tasa vefa wehlc Balam
Date: August 12 - 22

Original Purpose: He makes men invisible and witty and can tell the past, present and future.

Author's Notes: Invoke Balam to get over social awkwardness or to find the inner reasons for shyness or discomfort. Leave a piece of gold in offering to Balam (and his sigil) on the altar to keep magickal works secret until they manifest the desired results.

Week 51 - Balam- Meditation

Today while drawing the sigil of Balam I want you to think about your confidence - specifically in social situations. Draw the seal, think on this, and jot down any keywords that come to mind that you'd like to explore in your Freewrite tomorrow.

Week 51 - Balam - Freewrite

With today's freewrite, I want you to take all those keywords you came up with during your meditation and use them as writing prompts. You can do association. You can write about a time you felt socially confidence or a time you wanted to disappear. Also ask yourself a few questions about your confidence in social situations. Are you more or less confident in a group of strangers vs. a group of friends? Do you like to people watch and wish you could just melt into the background and observe? Or is that your usual MO? Confront those socially awkward situations in life where you embarrassed yourself and you wanted to hide under a rock by writing about them. Feel that embarrassment again. Sometimes confronting our own social awkwardness makes us realize it's not as bad as we thought. Other times it may reveal you're holding yourself back from being able to network or go further socially or in your career. Note that Balam is also great to help diviners hone their skills. You're welcome to focus on that this week, instead if you need a break from the shadow work.

Week 51 - Balam- Dreamwork

Tonight, I want you to go into your dream state affirming that you ARE NOT socially awkward, and that you do have the confidence. Or that you're a badass seer. What do you dream of going into sleep with the intent to be the person you want to be with regard to these particular areas? Be sure to write down your dreams and consider all symbology. Yes, you can use dream dictionaries for this, but I've found that oftentimes people already have their own ideas of what symbols mean. For me, dreaming of cats always foretells the publishing success of something. It might be time to consider creating a dream dictionary of your dreams' own personal symbology. You'll find It easier to do if you journal your dreams to help you find patterns and compare it with what happened in your everyday life.

Week 51 - Balam - Invocation/Evocation #1

If you can find a social event to attend this week - I want you to invoke or evoke Balam before you attend the event drawing Balam's energy into you for either confidence OR invisibility to see if you can manifest the desired result. Be sure to jot any notes or observations into your journal when you return home, when your thoughts are fresh. You may also use today's ritual time to do some divination.

Week 51 - Balam - Invocation/Evocation #2

Repeat yesterday's Invocation/Evocation or do a request ritual for Balam to bring you confidence, invisibility, or to help you manifest better divination skills. This is basically a fancy way of saying — do your own thing today!

Week 51 - Balam- Create a Spell or Ritual

Today I want you to make a gold charm that will be a permanent magickal artifact in your magickal arsenal. It can be a gold charm blessed by Balam and left on the altar to keep your work hidden from others, or it can take the form of a necklace or piece of jewelry you wear to hide yourself in a crowd (for people watching).

Week 51 - Balam - Rest/Reflect/Plan/Meditate

What did Balam teach you? Especially if you experience social anxiety or awkwardness in crowds of people. What can you work on going forward to get where you want to be? Or are you comfortable where you're at socially?

WEEK 52: ALLOCES

DUKE
Color: Green
Incense: Sandalwood
Metal: Copper
Planet: Venus
Element: Fire
Enn: Typan efna Alloces met tasa
Date: August 23 – September 1

Original Purpose: Astronomy and drawing familiars.

Author's Notes: Invoke for helping one focus, to establish clear thinking and boundaries, and to build foundations. Some believe Alloces to be a Daemon of clay and metal artists as well as architects.

Week 52 - Alloces - Meditation

This week, during your meditation, I want you to ground yourself. Visualize the sigil and let that sigil sit in your mind and build foundation. Let it inspire your creativity. Draw the sigil. Paint the sigil. Make a sculpture of the sigil. Carve it or burn it into wood. Take a deep breath and focus on your breath for a while.

Week 52 - Alloces - Freewrite

You can use this freewrite to explore what you ask your familiar to do. To ask yourself if you need more familiars. Or you can use this freewrite to ask yourself what you need right now to build a strong foundation, and to inspire you. What inspires you? Are there any boundaries you need to establish right now? What knowledge do you need to move forward? What brings you clear thought and creative comfort? Is it time to revamp your studio/office/creative space? Is it time to make a plan? What can you do this week that will help you move into the coming months standing on solid ground?

Week 52 - Alloces- Dreamwork

Tonight, just focus on the sigil as you fall asleep and see what comes of it. Do you have a vision? A thought? A dream? Sometimes we get nothing from the dreamwork, but while we're awake the next day - something comes to us with such incredible inspiration that it haunts us. Be sure to leave space in your journals for anything that haunts you or occurs to you tomorrow - even if it didn't manifest as a dream.

Week 52 - Alloces - Invocation/Evocation #1

Choose one of the following: Invoke Alloces and:
1. Create a piece of artwork.
2. Make a list of goals for the coming months and burn them in the offering bowl, thus throwing your intent into the universe.
3. Draw the Daemon into you and ask it for stability or inspiration.

Week 52 - Alloces - Invocation/Evocation #2

Choose one of the following: Invoke Alloces and:
1. Do a divination session to ask the Daemon what you should focus on in the coming year.
2. Draw the Daemonic into you and ask for stability and inspiration.

Week 52 - Alloces - Create a Spell or Ritual

Just create. Really - this is a free day where you get to do whatever you feel inspired to do, even if it's just sitting on the couch binge watching your favorite show. At the end of the day, write a paragraph about what doing this manifested for you. Did having a day off manifest rest and well-being? Did going to a show with a friend manifest memories? Did going to work manifest more financial security? You get the gist.

Week 52 - Alloces - Rest/Reflect/Plan/Meditate

What did Alloces teach you about your process? About what you manifest? About your foundation and/or boundaries? About what you need to learn in order to move forward?

WEEK 53: CAMIO/CAIM

PRESIDENT
Color: Orange
Incense: Storax
Metal: Mercury
Planet: Mercury
Element: Fire
Enn: (also Caim) – Tasa on ca Caim renich
Date: September 2 -11

Original Purpose: He can be sought using pyromancy. He can argue your case or help you understand animals. He gives answers of things to come.

Author's Notes: I actually know a veterinarian who wore the sigil of Camio. He believed it helped him to understand the needs of his patients better. Camio can be invoked for divination of any type. Wear his sigil to see into any situation you encounter.

Week 53 - Camio - Meditation

As you're doing today's meditation, maybe focusing on the sigil, or on the Daemonic force itself, I want you to consider your pets or issues where you might require bright flashes of insight. Also consider your divination methods.

Week 53 - Camio - Freewrite

For today's exercise - write about your animal companions and your connection with them. Are any of them familiars? (By familiar I mean do you utilize them as you would a familiar by asking them to do things for you like gathering information, bringing you opportunities, etc.?) Oftentimes when people call their animal a familiar, they just mean the it likes to hang out while they're doing ritual work. The scope of the actual familiar is quite broader than that. If your animals could talk to you, what would they say? Can you communicate with them? If you don't have animal companions, it may be time to write up an assessment of your intuition and skills with divination. How do you feel about divination as a whole? How do you view your intuition? Do you listen to it?

Week 53 - Camio- Dreamwork

Tonight, I want you to do a short visualization before you go to sleep. Make sure the Daemon's seal is beneath your pillow or mattress, or somewhere you can see it if you prefer. I want you to visualize the sigil, and then visualize your animal companion(s) (one at a time if you have more than one) and I want you to fall asleep with the intention of having Camio come to you through your animal companion. What does this exercise produce, if anything? If you don't get a result, don't beat yourself up. It's just an experiment. All magick is experimentation. If you did dream of your pet speaking to you - do your best to write down what it said (or an approximation) in your dream journal.

Week 53 - Camio - Invocation/Evocation #1

Today, invoke Camio in the presence of your animal companion(s) and simply ask that you are better able to communicate with your animals. How does the animal react to this ritual?

Alternatively, invoke Camio and do a fire scrying session in a candle flame. Be sure to make any notes about anything you see, feel, or "hear" in your journal.

Week 53 - Camio - Invocation/Evocation #2

Today, I want you to create a list of questions you need answers to, then invoke Camio and perform a scrying session, asking each question and carefully recording each answer you get. You can use a mirror, water, ink, flame, or whichever method you like. If you want to use a spirit board (prepared for Daemonic communication as in Drawing Down Belial) or pendulum, you can do that, too. But afterward, as you're writing up your results, I want you to pay particular attention to how any visions, smells, sounds, or insights manifested. Again, note any behavior of your animal companions during the ritual. The main point of this ritual is to really pay attention to HOW your divination skills feel and manifest. How does this particular Daemon feel to you?

Week 53 - Camio- Create a Spell or Ritual

Create a spell or ritual working with Camio to:

1. Draw familiars to you.
2. To make a pet a familiar.
3. To draw the power of Camio into your divination sessions.

Week 53 - Camio - Rest/Reflect/Plan/Meditate

What did this week teach you about your animal companions? What lessons did Camio have for you about communicating with animals? What did Camio teach you about your particular set of divination skills? What insights manifested for you?

Is Camio a Daemon you feel comfortable with? Are you likely to work with Camio again?

WEEK 54: MURMUR

DUKE
Color: Green
Incense: Sandalwood
Metal: Copper
Planet: Venus
Element: Water Fire
Enn: (also Murmus)- Vefa mena Murmur ayer
Date: September 12 - 22

Original Purpose: (Also listed as an Earl) Teaches philosophy and can be invoked for necromancy.

Author's Notes: Murmur can keep the dead from harming the living or overstaying its welcome in possessing a medium during channeling sessions. Murmur, for me, was one of the more aggressive and intimidating necromantic Daemons of the Goetia.

Week 54 - Murmur - Meditation

Murmur has the alchemical function of dissolution; in that he dissolves the veil between the living and the dead. But it's also prudent to remember that

Death Daemons are also Daemons of change and adaptation. So, if he can dissolve veils between worlds, he can also dissolve obstacles and challenges, or barriers keeping you from making changes or moving forward in stalled situations. As you draw his sigil and meditate on Murmur, think of what needs dissolution in your life. What obstacles, attitudes, beliefs need to be removed? Think of it as breaking things down so one can start over rebuilding.

Week 54 - Murmur- Freewrite

Now, on all the things you meditated on yesterday - write down your feelings about it today. What needs to dissolve? A bad habit? The ties that bind you to a toxic person? Your thinking about work or a relationship? An obstacle? Make a list if you have more than one thing. Of course, you can also write about your feelings about death and change or write about someone you loved who has died. How do you feel after this writing exercise? Sometimes tapping deep emotional areas, like death, can be exhausting. If you find you're tired after this exercise, be kind to yourself and either rest or take a walk. Or balance yourself.

Week 54 - Murmur- Dreamwork

Today, I want you to go to sleep visualizing yourself dissolving a bad habit or feeling. Or a person you'd like to remove from your life. Or anything else you can visualize dissolving. Maybe it's an obstacle. What comes of this? Did you have a dream? How did you feel when you woke up? What was the quality of your sleep?

Week 54 - Murmur - Invocation/Evocation #1

Today I want you to invoke Murmur, ask him to help you dissolve all negativity, and do a complete space cleansing/banishment, dissolution of negative energy throughout your home. Burn sage or frankincense. Sprinkle blessed or consecrated water. Anoint the doors with a cleansing or banishment oleum. Asperge with rosemary or another herb of your choice. Do whatever "feels" intuitively right to you to cleanse your space and dissolve all negativity with the assistance of Murmur. You might consider lighting a black charm candle to help absorb any leftover negativity so it can burn it away.

You are also welcome to try a necromancy session to speak to a deceased loved one by invoking Murmur and asking him to bring forward your loved one so you can communicate with them via the scrying mirror or using a prepared spirit board (see *Drawing Down Belial* for how to prepare a board).

Week 54 - Murmur - Invocation/Evocation #2

For today's invocation exercise - invoke Murmur (or evoke as the case may be) and draw that energy of dissolution through you to dissolve negative feelings and urges, or to remove obstacles. You're also welcome to do a divination or ascension session with Murmur depending on how you tolerate him.

Murmur can be a bit intimidating for some people. If you run across a Daemon like this, and working with that Daemonic energy causes you negative feelings/symptoms, you are welcome to sit these exercises out and just meditate on the alchemical process of dissolution and self-transformation. Keep that in mind for all 72 Daemons. It's perfectly okay to not follow every prescribed exercise.

Week 54 - Murmur - Create a Spell or Ritual

For today's spell/ritual or magickal item or talisman in the name of Murmur - consider:

1. A spell or ritual to speak with the Dead with Murmur's assistance.
2. A talisman for transformation.
3. Something to remove obstacles with Murmur's help.
4. An exorcism or banishing ritual utilizing Murmur's help.

Week 54 - Murmur - Rest/Reflect/Plan/Meditate

How did your energy mesh with Murmur's? Is this a Daemonic force you'll work with again? Is he on your go-to list for a particular purpose? How did you feel after working with him? Energized? Grounded? Tired? Sick? How was your mental acuity after working with Murmur? How did your energy vibration feel? What did this past week teach you about yourself, the Daemon, and the world around you?

WEEK 55: OROBAS

PRINCE
Color: Blue
Incense: Cedar
Metal: Tin
Planet: Jupiter
Element: Water
Enn: Jedan tasa hoet naca Orobas
Date: September 23 – October 2

Original Purpose: Divination, gives dignities and favors of both friends and enemies. He also tell you the nature of the divine and the universe. The Goetia tells us he is very faithful to the magician who invokes him.

Author's Notes: Excellent to invoke for bindings and changing people's opinions. Orobas is a Daemon of wisdom. His energy is very calming. He reminded me of a tamer version of Leviathan.

See information about Orobas vs. Ouroboros in the appendices.

Week 55 - Orobas - Meditation

Today while meditating on Orobas and drawing his seal, think about how you can transform yourself. Think about the snake devouring its tail for infinity. The never-ending circle of life. The cycles of everything. But mostly, I want you to try to calm yourself and be aware of your stress levels and use this meditation to calm yourself.

Week 55 - Orobas - Freewrite

What traits of yours would you like to amplify? Which traits are your best traits? If you were someone else, what would you say they most admired about you? What are your strengths? What are your weaknesses? In what areas can you transform yourself to be better? If this line of thinking doesn't inspire this freewriting session, think about whose opinions you need to alter and how. Think about what self-care you need right now. Write about the knowledge or wisdom you could use right now to make something (a relationship, project, or situation) easier on you. What could you bind to help you move forward? Remember that binding isn't just for people, but also situations, bad habits, and even thought patterns.

Remember that the freewriting exercise is meant to help you to explore yourself, your environment, and your life at this very moment - as well as people and situations in your life. It's meant to help you understand your emotions and feelings, and find areas for self-work and shadow work, and presumably areas where the Daemonic Divine can intervene and help you make meaningful change. The more control we exercise over our thoughts, actions, words, and emotions - the easier it becomes to manifest change in our lives in ways that make our lives more authentic and meaningful - as well as fulfilling.

Week 55 - Orobas- Dreamwork

Tonight, visualize Orobas' seal as you fall asleep. But I want you to go into sleep with the intention of actually getting a solid night of restful sleep.
How was your rest? Do you feel refreshed when you wake up? Did you have any dreams or wake up with any thoughts popping into your head? Again, it's okay if nothing happened.

Week 55 - Orobas- Invocation/Evocation #1

Today, I want you to invoke Orobas and then perform one of the following:

1. A request ritual, requesting something Orobas is good at.
2. A divination session.
3. An elemental balancing or drawing the spirit through you for the calming effect (if you find

Orobas calming).

Week 55 - Orobas- Invocation/Evocation #2

Today, invoke Orobas until the energy/vibration of the room changes. Then, on a piece of paper I want you to write down all your negative thoughts, fears and habits in black ink. With red ink, draw Orobas' seal over that. Roll up the piece of paper into a "scroll". Then, with black yarn, thread, or twine - bind the scroll, visualizing Orobas helping you to bind all of these things that could potentially be holding you back.

Leave space in your journal to later record the effects of this ritual.

Week 55 - Orobas - Create a Spell or Ritual

Today, create a spell or ritual, or magickal artifact in the name of Orobas for one of the following:

1. An talisman to cause you to transform into your best self (to glamor others)
2. A spell or ritual for divination.
3. A spa day ritual for relaxation.
4. A binding in the name of Orobas.

Week 55 - Orobas- Rest/Reflect/Plan/Meditate

How do you feel about Orobas? Do you think Orobas is a Daemonic force you could work with again? How was the working relationship by day 6? What did the Daemon teach you? About the Daemon? About yourself? Was this a relatively calm week for you? Or did you feel anxious or agitated?

WEEK 56: GREMORY

DUKE
Color: Green
Incense: Sandalwood
Metal: Copper
Planet: Venus
Element: Water
Enn: (also Gemory or Gamori) – An tasa shi Gremory on ca
Date: October 3 - 12

Original Purpose: She can be invoked for divination, to find hidden treasures, and to invoke the love of women.

Author's Notes: To learn Magick. Some say Gremory is akin to Delepitorae or Seshat, only less intense. I invoked Gremory to find a lost item and strangely it appeared in a place I had searched thoroughly three times.

Week 56 - Gremory - Meditation

As you draw Gremory's seal today, I'd like you to think about what you still feel you need to learn about magick and divination. If you're looking for a partner, visualize the partner you'd like. If you have a partner, think about the state of the relationship. Alternatively, perhaps you've lost something. It doesn't have to be a physical object. It could be your enjoyment of something, or your passion or motivation. These are all things you can ruminate over while you consider Gremory. Or - just spend time with the sigil and the Daemon, considering its nature.

Week 56 - Gremory- Freewrite

Today, you get to choose which prompt you want to start your freewrite with. Will it be your thoughts on relationships? The art of love magick? Or perhaps it will be a list of all the things about magick and divination you'd like to learn. Maybe you want to focus on something you feel you've lost over the years, because Gremory is rather adept at helping people find missing things (whether physical, emotional, mental, etc.). He gives great advice so listen and write down anything you may "hear" or think as you're doing the freewriting exercise.

I am often asked if people can use the freewriting exercise to do some automatic writing while channeling the Daemon, and the answer is absolutely. So, if you'd like to try that instead - Gremory is a great Daemon to practice this with.

Week 56 - Gremory- Dreamwork

Tonight, go into sleep focusing on the Daemons seal and finding something lost, or learning something new. Keep an open mind. Be sure to write up anything you remember from your dreams upon waking, or anything that occurs to you in the 12 hours after you wake up. Sometimes insights aren't always instantaneous. They take time to develop and reveal themselves.

Week 56 - Gremory- Invocation/Evocation #1

Today, choose one of the following for your invocation:

1. Goetic style scrying session (or other divination).
2. A Daemonolatry style request ritual.
3. A ritual to draw more love into your life.
4. An ascension session.

Week 56 - Gremory - Invocation/Evocation #2

Today, choose a different reason for Invocation, or create your own.
1. Goetic style scrying session (or other divination).
2. A Daemonolatry style request ritual.
3. A ritual to draw more love into your life.

4. An ascension session.

Week 56 - Gremory - Create a Spell or Ritual

You may wonder why I ask you to create your own spells or rituals and the reason is simple — this is an advanced exercise. The reason there are not so many "advanced" books is because people don't realize that advanced practitioners carve their own path and write their own ritual. One of the most advanced books I've written is *The Art of Creative Magick*, and yet I recommend it to beginners.

So today, create your own spell, ritual, or magickal item for one of the following reasons:

1. A love spell utilizing Gremory's influence.
2. An item to help you find lost things.
3. A ritual for divination with Gremory.

Week 56 - Gremory – Rest / Reflect / Plan / Meditate

In what ways did Gremory help you this week? What wisdom did this Daemon impart to you? Do you feel a bit wiser? How much work remains to be done? Will Gremory have a place in Daemons you work with in the future? Be sure to note any distinguishing feelings, smells, energy signatures that you noticed that are unique to Gremory. You should be doing this for all the Daemons, but by now, 56 weeks in, you should really be feeling the differences between them and developing some discernment.

WEEK 57: OSE

PRESIDENT
Color: Orange
Incense: Storax
Metal: Mercury
Planet: Mercury
Element: Air
Enn: (also Voso or Oso) – Ayer serpente Ose
Date: October 12 - 22

Original Purpose: Can change a man into any form. Can give answers about things hidden and divine (i.e. occult).

Author's Notes: To learn foreign languages or to pick up on computer or workplace skills. Also work with Ose when working magick for other people. It will help open them up to changes (especially changes in thought or opinion).

Week 57 - Ose - Meditation

Today, as you're drawing Ose's sigil and meditating on this Daemonic force, I want you to keep in mind uncovering that which is hidden, higher education (workplace type skills especially), personal transformation or shapeshifting, and your own adaptability to change. As an exercise here, visualize yourself changing from human form to something else and back again in presence of the Daemon. That's an exercise for more advanced practitioners, but I have confidence most of you reading this can do it.

Week 57 - Ose - Freewrite

Today's Writing Prompts: What do you need to learn to further your career or improve your current work/career situation? What hidden things do you need to uncover? It could be someone's motivation, or maybe how others view you. If you could shapeshift into anything, what would you shift into and why? Finally - how adaptable are you to change? How could learning to shapeshift change your thinking, or help you become more adaptable?

Week 57 - Ose- Dreamwork

Tonight, as you're drifting off to sleep, I want you to visualize or imagine a natural setting, then visualize yourself shifting into an animal of your choice and running through that natural environment (whether forest, desert, water, lake, plains, etc.). Fall asleep to this visualization. Does it carry over into the dream world? Did you meet or speak to anyone in your dreams? How was the quality of your sleep? How did the visualization of "shifting" feel? Note any revelations that came from this exercise.

Week 57 - Ose - Invocation/Evocation #1

Today, I want you to invoke/evoke Ose and then draw the Daemonic energy into you and then SHIFT your perspective on something you need to adapt to. For example - if you're really angry about something, shift your perspective and see if you can adapt to the situation, thus removing the anger. You can do this with things you're sad about. Or things you wish were different. You can also use this invocation exercise to adapt to major life changes like a change in career, end of career, marriage, death, new baby, empty nester, etc.

If this exercise doesn't work for you - try shifting into a more confident version of yourself. Invoke the Daemon and shift into someone who is more outspoken, eloquent, vibrant, or beautiful. How you shapeshift is literally up to you.

Try creating a sigil of Ose and infusing it with shapeshifting energy. Then carry it with you to shapeshift into anything you wish at any time.

Week 57 - Ose - Invocation/Evocation #2

Today, do an invocation/evocation and speak with Ose through the black mirror (crystals, spirit boards, and both water and fire scrying can be used, too, if one of those is your preference). What does Ose reveal to you? Be sure to write up a detailed result.

You're also welcome to do a ritual of your choice.

Week 57 - Ose - Create a Spell or Ritual

With the aid of Ose create one of the following:
1. A talisman to help you focus while studying.
2. A spell to shapeshift.
3. A ritual to reveal what is hidden.

Week 57 - Ose - Rest/Reflect/Plan/Meditate

What did Ose teach you about your adaptability? Did you learn any skills you need to learn? Does Ose help you focus during study? Did you enjoy shapeshifting? What did Ose have to offer? Did your energy mesh with Ose? Rate this Daemon on a scale of 1-5 (or 1-10 if you prefer) where one is "I'd never work with this Daemon again" to 5 (or 10) where five is "I want to work with this Daemon more often and may add them to my personal pantheon."

WEEK 58: AMY

PRESIDENT
Color: Orange
Incense: Storax
Metal: Mercury
Planet: Mercury
Element: Fire
Enn: (also Avnas) – Tu Fubin Amy secore
Date: October 23 – November 1

Original Purpose: Can teach you liberal sciences and astrology. Gives good familiars and can give treasure kept by spirits.

Author's Notes: The spark of divinatory fire. Amy is a seer's Daemon. If you are seeking to learn about making magickal talismans, or need sigils or enns and have had difficulty getting information from other Daemons, work with Amy and your chances to get these things will increase.

Week 58 - Amy- Meditation

Focus on Amy's sigil while thinking of this Daemonic force. As you draw it, follow your intuition and add or delete from the sigil as you see fit. If you feel like drawing a completely different shape, do that. What symbols are pleasing to Amy? Do you see anything in your mind's eye? Be sure to note this as you focus on Amy for this meditation.

Some of you may be choosing to do an ascension exercise as your meditation, or something else, but do try allowing the Daemonic to show you symbols and modify sigils. You'll understand once you do your freewrite exercise tomorrow.

Week 58 - Amy - Freewrite

Amy is a Daemon who can help you divine variant sigils and enns that are personal connections between you and the Daemonic forces you're working with, and can bring other spirits forward for you to communicate with. Those who are new to Daemonic communication often credit Amy with being one of the easier spirits to make contact with. Amy can also help the magician learn astrology, conjure familiars, and get things moving (sometimes by teaching energy work). All of this said — today I want you to do a freewrite where you just draw or write whatever comes to mind. Let the Daemonic force Amy guide you.

Week 58 - Amy- Dreamwork

Tonight, I want you to spend a few minutes in meditation on Amy's sigil before bed. Then just go to sleep as you normally would. When you wake, write up anything that came of your dreams. Note your quality and duration of sleep and your energy level upon waking.

Again, noting these things can tell you which Daemons drain you and which Daemons energize you.

Week 58 - Amy - Invocation/Evocation #1

Today we're going to do an exercise that's great to perform with a group of fellow practitioners. Invoke Amy in the style to which you are accustomed. You can also vibrate the enn until the energy in the room changes. Now, on a piece of paper, I want you to focus on Amy and ask the Daemon to give you a sigil for them that will link you to Amy. Draw what you see or hear. This is almost like an automatic writing session but instead of drawing the Daemonic force through you, you're listening and paying attention. Draw the symbol. Or write the words. Or whatever you get.
Be sure to note how the invocation made you feel. Your energy levels. Etc.

Week 58 - Amy - Invocation/Evocation #2

Today, take the symbol you got in yesterday's Invocation and burn it into wood, carve it into wood, stone, or clay, or find a way to make a more permanent Daemonic sigil that you can use during your ritual work with Amy. Imbue it with the powers of sight, energy, communication, and helpers. Or whatever else Amy and Amy's energy represent to you.

Afterward, do a request asking the Daemon to bring you energy or familiars. Carry the seal with you the rest of the week or keep it somewhere where you can see it all week.

Be sure to leave space in your journal to write your results with this exercise (and any subsequent work you might do with Amy using this seal).

Week 58 - Amy - Create a Spell or Ritual

1. Create a ritual utilizing Amy's energy to get things moving.
2. Create a magickal item that will give you a burst of energy when you're low.
3. Create a spell or ritual to draw familiars via Amy.
4. Create a ritual to have Amy bring other spirits forward so you can speak with them via your preferred divination method.

Week 58 - Amy - Rest/Reflect/Plan/Meditate

I know a week isn't a lot of time to fully test some of the magickal artifacts you'll make during this immersion, or to test the sigils and enns you may get from the Daemons you're working with. However, I do want you to write down how things went with your sigil. If you feel comfortable doing so, share your sigil with others who have done the same exercise and note any similarities. I've done this comparison in multiple study groups in the past and it is always surprising how often different sigils gotten from different people have common patterns. Did you work well with Amy? Did this work inspire you to want to plan more work with Amy in the future?

WEEK 59: ORIAS

MARQUIS
Color: Violet
Incense: Jasmine
Metal: Silver
Planet: Moon
Element: Air
Enn: (also Oriax) – Lirach mena Orias Anay na
Date: November 2 - 12

Original Purpose: Teaches astronomy, astrology, and transforms men. He can also give you favor with friends or enemies.

Author's Notes: To make transformations to the self (i.e., the physical body). Orias can help you get physically fit and healthy. I kind of view him as a personal trainer for one's willpower.

Week 59 - Orias - Meditation

Today as you draw Orias' sigil (or trace it if you wish), I want you to think about your mental wellbeing and your emotional state. Just focus on being calm and at peace. If you find yourself getting stressed or agitated, or your mind wandering, focus on your breath.

Another meditation exercise you might try is to hold your hands over places on your body that need healing, or over your heart if you need emotional healing. Visualize the Daemon's sigil blazing white and blue in the palms of your hands and radiating healing energy outward. Use this meditation time for healing energy work and visualization.

Week 59 - Orias- Freewrite

Today, let's get it all out. I want you to write about an emotional trauma you've experienced. Allow yourself to feel the pain and anger. Accept that pain and anger are part of the process of dealing with emotional trauma. Write down what happened in explicit detail - enough detail to evoke those same emotions from you. Do this for as long as you can stand it.

For some people, the act of writing it out is enough. For others, burning what was written as a symbolic "this no longer defines me or holds me prisoner" is more cathartic. Do whatever feels right to you right here. If you need to rip out the pages of the journal and burn them, do it. If you just need to close the journal and walk away - do that. The point is to get it out onto paper. Accept that this happened. Accept how it made you feel. Accept that it is part of you but doesn't need to define you and hold you back.

As you may have guessed - Orias is all about mental well-being and transformation. Healing from emotional traumas. Orias can also help us transform friendships in ways that are more meaningful and deeper. Orias can boost your confidence after emotional trauma as well. Completely unrelated, for the astrologers among you, Orias can help you with learning astrology, so if you're not ready to face any emotional healing or well-being this week, you're welcome to study Astrology because you'll be very likely to retain what you're learning right now. And Orias may offer some insight into your own relationship with the astrological signs and influences affecting you now.

Week 59 - Orias- Dreamwork

Because this week is another "self-care" week, tonight I still want you to sleep with Orias' seal in sight or beneath your mattress or pillow - but I want you to focus on getting the best night's rest you can get. Use a lavender linen spray or essential oil in your bedroom. Take a warm bath or shower before bed to relax you. Have your partner give you a massage or do self-massage.
Don't forget to take notes about how you slept, for how long, and how rested and refreshed you feel upon waking on top of any dreams you had or any

thoughts you had upon waking. The Daemonic is always communicating with us. Sometimes it's just a matter of whether or not we're listening. So be still and listen. The Daemonic doesn't always scream or manifest in bright flashes of light. Sometimes the message is gentle or subtle, like a whisper in the breeze.

Week 59 - Orias - Invocation/Evocation #1

Tonight, I want you to vibrate the enn until the energy in the room changes, then I want you to write a simple request on a piece of paper: Orias, bring me emotional healing, confidence, and peace. Then sign your name, draw the seal of the Daemon. If you're a Daemonolater, add a drop of blood. If you're not, it may be best you don't do blood magick, especially if you have any hangups or fears surrounding blood magick. Then burn the paper in the offering bowl and spend at least 10 minutes afterward in silent meditation or energy work like qi gong. Thank the Daemon for being present, close your ritual, and go about the rest of your day/evening.

Week 59 - Orias - Invocation/Evocation #2

Today, I want you to invoke/evoke Orias and draw Orias' energy into you. Change your vibration to

Orias' if you can. Then visualize that energy transforming and healing you from the inside out. You're also welcome to do a divination or work for friendship if you prefer.

But if you do the healing work where you draw the Daemonic force into you and visualize intense emotional healing by activating those emotions needing to be healed, I want you to leave space in your journal to write up how you feel 24 hours after this ritual. Do you feel stronger? More confident? Like something has shifted? This is actually a great exercise if you're battling depression or deep-seated anger. Orias can help transform your emotional state from trauma to something that better serves you. This is also why a lot of people work with Orias for weight loss. Because most people have emotional triggers behind their over-eating, or emotional issues behind their body image and Orias can help them address those emotional triggers and promote healing, thus weight loss.

Week 59 - Orias - Create a Spell or Ritual

Today, create a spell or ritual with Orias (or create a magickal artifact if you wish) for one of the following:

1. For weight loss.
2. For confidence.
3. For emotional healing.

4. For mental well-being (something that helps curb anxiety maybe)
5. To draw friends who are right for you at this time.

Week 59 - Orias - Rest/Reflect/Plan/Meditate

How do you feel about Orias overall? Was this Daemon useful in helping you heal? Would you work with him further in this area? Did this Daemonic force inspire you? Your relationship with Orias is unique to you and you should note any striking things you noticed during your week with them. Don't forget to include all the senses and how the Daemon manipulated your senses. What did their vibration feel like? How did you feel before, during, and after your work with them? What shadow work manifested from this week?

WEEK 60: VAPULA

DUKE
Color: Green
Incense: Sandalwood
Metal: Copper
Planet: Venus
Element: Air
Enn: (also Naphula) – Renich secore Vapula typan
Date: November 13 - 22

Original Purpose: Can make one knowledgeable in crafts and sciences.

Author's Notes: Invoke for creative business endeavors or when seeking creative inspiration. I found Vapula a bit stand-offish and untrusting. It took me five workings for Vapula to finally come forth and show me her true nature.

I had a very crafty friend in Texas who put the seal of Vapula on her craft room wall and always referred to Vapula as her "arts and crafts Daemon". So, if you're a crafty person - this Daemon might become the Matron of your craft room, too!

Week 60 - Vapula - Meditation

This will be a good week to reflect on what inspires you and how you exercise your creativity. This also includes how your creativity manifests in your magickal work, and even in your career and personal life. Creativity isn't just arts and crafts. Scientists and engineers are creative people, too, in that they're creative problem solvers. So as you're doing your meditation today, drawing the seal and focusing on Vapula overall, consider how the energy of Vapula plays a role in your life. What does your inner Vapula tell you about your creative process?

Week 60 - Vapula - Freewrite

Now that you have started contemplating your creativity and inspiration in conjunction with Vapula, today, I want you to put it to paper. What would inspire you today? Which creative pursuits are you happiest while pursuing? Are you a creative problem solver? Which problems need creative solutions? What do you need to create or craft to manifest what you need?

Week 60 - Vapula- Dreamwork

Tonight, think of the sigil and enn of Vapula as you fall asleep. Enter sleep open-minded and allow whatever. Yes, you can go into sleep having a firm idea of what you want to know or learn, or with a specific intent, but for more creative divine intelligences, sometimes it's best to go into sleep with an open mind.

Week 60 - Vapula - Invocation/Evocation #1

If you are a crafter or a creative:

I want you to invoke Vapula in your craft area/space/room AND hang Vapula's sigil in this room. Leave space in your journal here so you can reflect on this after a few weeks time. Some questions to ask yourself - did my productivity increase? Did I feel more inspired or more creative? Was I drawn to my creative space more often?

If you are looking for creative solutions to a problem:

Invoke Vapula and do a standard request ritual (see *The Complete Book of Demonolatry*) for the format of a standard request ritual. Ask for a solution to the problem. Burn it in the offering bowl. Thank Vapula, close the ritual, and go about your business.

Week 60 - Vapula- Invocation/Evocation #2

Today, I want you to invoke Vapula and perform a scrying session with the Daemon and just see what comes of it. You may go into the session with a list of questions, or just go in with an open mind and a willingness to learn. Either way, bring your journal or a pad of paper so you can take notes. Daemons tend to be rather patient and will pause to let you write stuff down.

Alternatively, invoke Vapula, draw the Daemonic energy into you (empowering your internal Vapula) and do some automatic writing or drawing.

Week 60 - Vapula - Create a Spell or Ritual

Create a Spell or Ritual (or magickal artifact) this week for:

1. Inspiration
2. A consecrated sigil of Vapula for your creative space/area to draw inspiration
3. To build a crafting skill.
4. To solve problems.

Week 60 - Vapula - Rest/Reflect/Plan/Meditate

Did you find work with Vapula inspiring? Did you learn anything about yourself or the Daemon worth noting? Would you work with Vapula again?

Describe how you experienced Vapula's vibration and energy, Include sight, sound, smell, intuitive/psychic impressions, physical sensations, etc... If you created anything this week - what did you create and how do you feel about it? Be sure to write all of this down in your journal.

WEEK 61: ZAGAN

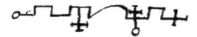

KING
Color: Yellow
Incense: Frankincense
Metal: Gold
Planet: Sun
Element: Earth
Enn: (also Zagam) Anay on ca secore Zagan tasa
Date: November 23 – December 2

Original Purpose: Daemon of transmutation and transformation. Can change anything into something else.

Author's Notes: Turns things into their opposites. Invoke to help curb addictions and bad habits or to make delusional people (or dabblers) see the truth. Zagam rites are a Demonolatry Keeper ritual.

Zagan, being a Daemon that changes things to their opposites - is one of those spirits that I encourage people to work with sparingly unless you need massive change. There is a way to temper the influence of these hard-hitting Daemons with gentler Daemons by working in tandem though. That said - this week you are going to work with Zagan in a gentle way that shouldn't cause too much discord. So, if the suggested exercises for this week seem gentle, that would be why. Please keep this in mind as you modify. Also, see the Appendices to this book for several articles about Zagan that you may find useful.

Week 61 - Zagan - Meditation

Today, just draw the sigil and "feel out" the Daemon. Consider various life changes you've had in the past, especially major ones. Think about what major life changes will come.

Week 61 - Zagan - Freewrite

Today I want you to write about how you deal with change. Are you adaptable? How much stress and anxiety does change cause you? How does stress manifest in YOU? For example, do you carry tension in your back? Your jaw? Do you emotionally lash out? Every person is different.

Week 61 - Zagan- Dreamwork

Tonight, I want you to go to sleep with the intention to meet with Zagan to talk. What kinds of dreams does this bring, if any? What kind of sleep does it produce? Did you have any ideas, thoughts, visions, or inclinations immediately upon waking? If so, write it all up in your dream journal.

Week 61 - Zagan - Invocation/Evocation #1

For beginners - Invoke Zagan and just sit with the Daemon's energy for a while.

For intermediate students - Invoke Zagan and do a request ritual for a SMALL change.

For advanced students - Invoke Zagan and do a scrying ritual to discuss with the Daemon changes that you might want to make.

Of course, regardless of your experience level, you're welcome to try any one of these. If you're short on time or lacking energy, simply meditating on Zagan is fine.

Week 61 - Zagan - Invocation/Evocation #2

For beginners - Invoke Zagan and do a request ritual for a small change.

For intermediate students - Invoke Zagan and draw the energy of Zagan into you. Mind you this may cause you to feel fear or anxiety or experience a physical reaction and your job will be to identify that reaction and WHY you had the reaction.

For advanced students - Invoke Zagan and go into ascension to speak with the Daemon about which path work needs to be done with regard to change.

Week 61 - Zagan - Create a Spell or Ritual

Create a spell, ritual, or magickal artifact with the influence of Zagan for one of the following:

1. For gentle, slow change.
2. For swift, abrupt change.
3. For adaptability.
4. For the power to change your situation at will. (i.e., a magickal enhancement for manifestation of will)

Week 61 - Zagan - Rest/Reflect/Plan/Meditate

How does Zagan's energy feel? What emotional reactions did you have to the work? What physical reactions did you experience? Do you feel like Zagan is a Daemon you would be able to work with as needed? Is this a Daemon you wouldn't work with? Why? Have your thoughts and feelings about change been altered during your week with Zagan? As always, you're welcome to come up with your own set of questions for reflection and meditation on each Daemonic force you're working with.

WEEK 62: VOLAC

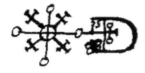

PRESIDENT
Color: Orange
Incense: Storax
Metal: Mercury
Planet: Mercury
Element: Earth
Enn: (also Valak, Valac, or Valu)– Avage Secore on ca Volac
Date: December 3 - 12

Original Purpose: Gives answers of where to find hidden treasures and can tell the magician where serpents are.

Author's Notes: Volac is the ultimate path-working Daemon of the Goetic hierarchy. Invoke him when you feel stuck in your spiritual growth or at a stalemate with your studies. Volac will point you in the right direction so you can find the wisdom and knowledge you seek.

Week 62- Volac - Meditation

The beauty of Volac, it seems, is just how different most people's experience working with Volac will be. Because we are all at different stages of growth in our lives, we all need different things, and have different areas we're working on, or struggling with. Even though Volac is a pathworking spirit. Volac is also very earthy and mercurial, meaning many of his lessons teach us how to think through what we're manifesting, and becoming aware of how our thinking manifests certain things in our lives. As you're doing today's meditation, I want you to consider your own role in your problems.

Week 62- Volac- Freewrite

Today I want you to brainstorm your entire spiritual journey. Summarize it. Write your story about how you chose an alternative (to mainstream) spirituality. Write about the major turning points - even if it's just a sentence highlighting each. Write about your journey and your pathworking so far. For some of you this may just be a few paragraphs. For others, you may feel like you can fill a book. Write as little or as much as you like about this. Then, when you're finished journaling today's thoughts, I want you to draw the seal of Volac at the bottom and leave it.

Week 62- Volac- Dreamwork

Tonight, I want you to go into sleep with the

intention of asking Volac to show you your next steps. What comes of this work? Remember, it's okay if you don't dream or have no results here. The intention of asking the Daemon to reveal an answer to you is out there and it's been my experience that we often receive answers swiftly, within 72 hours, no matter how subtle. So, keep your eyes open for guideposts and direction.

Week 62- Volac - Invocation/Evocation #1

Today, I want you to invoke Volac and perform a scrying session. Ask the Daemon to show you where you should look next. Be very aware of stray thoughts, feelings, images, sounds, smells, and physical sensations during this ritual. Be sure to write up everything you experience during this ritual.

Week 62- Volac - Invocation/Evocation #2

Today, invoke Volac and do a request ritual to ask Volac to bring opportunities that will further lead you to your Great Work. Leave space in your journal so you can note any opportunities that you feel arose from this particular ritual. Note that rituals like this also make us more hyper-aware of opportunities. Just because an opportunity presents itself doesn't mean anything will come of it UNLESS we choose to take the opportunity and do something with it.

Week 62- Volac - Create a Spell or Ritual

Today, create a spell, ritual, or magickal artifact with the energy of Volac for:

1. Drawing opportunities to further your Great Work.
2. To discover or uncover your Great Work.
3. To learn which path you should take (or make a choice between two paths)
4. For wisdom regarding your path.

Week 62- Volac - Rest/Reflect/Plan/Meditate

What did Volac reveal to you this week? I'm confident enough in Volac's efficacy that I expect everyone who did the work had something revealed to them (or a point driven home). What was it for you? How did Volac make you feel physically and emotionally? Did you experience any sober moments of extreme clarity this week? If so, write them down in your journal. What will you take away from your work with Volac? Will you work with Volac again?

WEEK 63: ANDRAS

MARQUIS
Color: Violet
Incense: Jasmine
Metal: Silver
Planet: Moon
Element: Air Fire
Enn: Entey ama Andras anay
Date: December 13 - 21

Original Purpose: His purpose is to cause calamity of all types.

Author's Notes: To help conceal the truth from others. Invoke Andras to resolve ongoing situations between people (usually by bringing them to a confrontation). While confrontation may not be desired, it will provide a quick resolution. You may invoke Andras with any Daemon of strength or influence to give you an edge in any situation where you feel you need it.

Week 63 - Andras - Meditation

A lot of people simply view Andras as an execration Daemon, or a Daemon they can work with to cause distraction or bring strength and influence to the magician. On top of that, however, he is also Airy/Fiery, with some Water aspects making him sought after for revealing or concealing the truth, and spirit communication. For execration, consider that vengeance often happens through forcing confrontation and bringing about resolution. While you're focusing on the seal (or drawing it), think about these things, or keep them loosely in your mind.

Week 63 - Andras - Freewrite

Today, write about a situation that needs resolution. Or what (or who) you need to confront in order to get things moving. It could be a person, or it could be a situation you've been avoiding, or a bad habit you've been engaging in. Hell, it could be a messy room in your home you've been meaning to clear out or reorganize. Write about confrontation. How do you react to confrontation? Why? How do you react to chaos and when things go wrong? Learning to navigate calamities and keep a cool head during any confrontation is a skill indeed. If you've already mastered these things (there may be some of you who have), consider working with Andras this week for spirit and other communication or strength and influence. In which case write about areas in your life and personality that could use strength. Write about communication. What areas of your life could be improved with better communication?

Week 63 - Andras- Dreamwork

Tonight, go into sleep thinking about communicating with Andras and gaining wisdom from him. He may even give you insight into where you should focus your invocations and ritual work for the rest of the week. As usual, write down everything you remember upon waking. Also watch for gentle nudges and cues during your waking hours in case the Daemon is communicating with you in more subtle ways.

Week 63 - Andras - Invocation/Evocation #1

Because Andras deals with revelation and communication - scrying rituals should be really strong with him. For your first invocation, call upon Andras using the enn until the vibration of the room changes, then perform a scrying session (use whichever scrying device you're comfortable with including mirrors, stones, your dark cell phone screen, fire, water — whatever) to speak with the Daemon and ask Andras to show you what you wish to know, or answer a prepared list of questions.

Week 63 - Andras- Invocation/Evocation #2

Today, you can either repeat yesterday's invocation, or you can use this invocation to do a request ritual where you ask the Daemon reveal or conceal something, or to give you strength/influence, or even to bring resolution through confrontation. Whichever you feel you need at this time. When you are finished burning the request in the offering bowl, thank Andras and close your ritual space.

Week 63 - Andras - Create a Spell or Ritual

Create a spell or ritual or magickal artifact utilizing the energy of Andras for:

1. Creating a new scrying mirror.
2. To become invisible.
3. To gain strength or influence over any situation.
4. To reveal secrets being kept from you.

Week 63 - Andras - Rest/Reflect/Plan/Meditate

What wisdom did Andras have for you this week? How did your energies mesh? Is this a Daemon you could see yourself working with further? If yes, why? If no, why not? What do you need to work on going forward? What was your favorite part of the previous week? The most difficult?

WEEK 64: FLAROS/HAURES

DUKE
Color: Green
Incense: Sandalwood
Metal: Copper
Planet: Venus
Element: Fire
Enn: (also Flaros, Flauros, Haurus, Flereous, or Havres) – Ganic tasa fubin Flauros.
Date: December 22 – 30

Original Purpose: He can destroy your enemies. He can tell you all things past, present, and future. He can tell you about divinity and the nature of the universe. Goetia warns that he is deceptive and unless forced into the triangle he will lie.

Author's Notes: Also, Flaros, associated with the Dukanté hierarchy as Flereous and twinned with Phenex/Phoenix (different aspects of similar energy). Fire baptisms. Starting a new phase in life or new projects or relationships.

Week 64- Haures - Meditation

This would be a great week to perform Fire baptisms if this is your wish. Also, if you need to open some roads (i.e., destroy blocks) or execration magick, you might start considering this now. This week is also prime for starting new things, building your confidence and energy/power as well as igniting passion, love, or lust. While Haures isn't one of the strongest "love/lust" Daemons and there are better ones to work with for such things, Haures (known as Flereous in the Dukanté hierarchy) can bring energy and excitement to relationships. Also, a great week to do energy work. I recommend some Tai Chi or Qi Gong to clear any blockages within your own energy. Consider all of this as you think about Haures and draw his seal during this meditation time.

Week 64- Haures - Freewrite

You can choose any or all of these questions as prompts for your freewrite, but also feel free to create your own. Remember that magick isn't about doing things by the book. It's about creation. You're a magician - create.

Is there anything blocking you? Where do you need a spark of activity right now? Have you attempted ascension? What are your feelings about the practice? How is your motivation? What would enhance it? What have you been putting off simply because you don't have the energy to do it? Can you do something to make a step toward starting something new this week?

Week 64- Haures- Dreamwork

Tonight, as you're falling asleep visualizing Haures' sigil (and even thinking the enn), I want you to travel to your astral temple and meet Haures there so he can give you a spark of energy that you can use any way you wish this week. One big burst of energy to help you do something you've been putting off or haven't had enough confidence to do. What comes of this exercise? Did you dream about the Daemon? What did Haures say to you? Recall everything you can and write it all down. Record every detail you can muster.

Week 64- Haures - Invocation/Evocation #1

Invoke Haures - visualize all the things standing in your way, gather your energy along with that of Haures, and then visualize blasting everything in your way off the face of the planet. You can also draw Haures' energy into you, then mesh it with your own and project it outward, growing and growing until it pushes everything negative from your space, and your life. These ritual visualizations can be very powerful. Be sure to drink plenty of water afterward and to note if working with such a strong Fire element makes you feel energetic or exhausted. Scatter brained? Or

Invoke Haures and cleanse your home and all your magickal paraphernalia of negative energy, visualizing all negativity being burned up.

Alternatively - consider invoking Haures for a personal Fire baptism ritual.

Week 64- Haures - Create a Spell or Ritual

Today, create a spell or ritual utilizing the energy of Haures for one of the following:

1. Drawing energy to you - for motivation.
2. Execration magick.
3. A ritual for a new beginning.
4. A spell to destroy blocks.
5. Your choice.

Week 64- Haures - Rest/Reflect/Plan/Meditate

How did you deal with the intense Fire energy of Haures this week? Was it too intense? Did you love it? Would you work with Haures again? Does your home and space feel more "active" and less stale than when you started the week? Did you find yourself more motivated to start something or finish it? Explore your thoughts, feelings, impressions, and interaction with this spirit in your journal.

WEEK 65: ANDREALPHUS

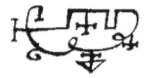

MARQUIS
Color: Violet
Incense: Jasmine
Metal: Silver
Planet: Moon
Element: Air
Enn: Mena Andrealphus tasa ramec ayer
Date: December 31 – January 9

Original Purpose: He can transform men into birds and teach astronomy and geometry.

Author's Notes: Andrealphus can be invoked to help dissolve magick or bring a situation to a close. If you want to seal something (a spell, a portal, or a situation), Andrealphus is also your Daemon for that.

Week 65 - Andrealphus - Meditation

As you're doing your meditation on Andrealphus today, I want you to think of ascension. Focus on your breath and the sigil, then attempt to visualize yourself floating. You may also choose to go to your astral temple and leave your body. But while you do this, carry Andrealphus' seal with you. One of Andrealphus' areas of specialty is to teach ascension and reveal higher consciousness.

Other areas you can mediate on include things you need closure on. Obstacles that need to be dissolved/removed. Protection (from the spirit world and psychic self-defense). Sealing portals to the spirit world. And finally, sealing magick. Which is like a period at the end of a sentence or the finality in one's tone at the end of a statement. Each spell or ritual has a point where you seal your intent (usually with your signature and the sigil of the spirit you may be working with) and you burn it in the offering bowl to release that intent into the universe. That's what sealing intent and/or sealing magick means in this instance.

Week 65 - Andrealphus - Freewrite

Today, write about your views of ascension and higher consciousness. Write about what sealing magick feels like. What sealing your intent feels like. Write about obstacles that could be dissolved, or what you need closure to. How are your skills of psychic self-defense?

Week 65 - Andrealphus - Dreamwork

Tonight, as you are falling asleep, take Andrealphus' seal with you to your astral temple and wait to sleep there. What happens? Be sure to write up anything you remember immediately upon waking.

Week 65 - Andrealphus - Invocation/Evocation #1

Today, we're going to invoke Andrealphus to clear negativity from our minds and to practice psychic self-defense. So first, vibrate the enn of Andrealphus until you feel the vibration in your head. Then visualize yourself standing in a circle of mirrors - all facing outward. On each mirror is the seal of Andrealphus (so it will help to attempt to commit the sigil to memory). Now visualize any negativity around you being sucked out of that circle (as if by a vacuum) into outer space just outside the circle of mirrors. As the energy tries to re-enter your space, it bounces off the mirror and can't get to you. If the negative energy comes from beyond the space outside the mirror, it is likely coming from a SOURCE. As it comes in and hits the mirror, practice mentally BOUNCING that energy back to its source. Do this for as long as you can stand it, and remember this technique, as it can be done anywhere and is a super useful tool in your arsenal to defend yourself against the psychic attacks of others (whether intentionally or not).

Week 65 - Andrealphus - Invocation/Evocation #2

Today, I want you to ascend to your astral temple, invoke Andrealphus there, and either talk with him, or bless and protect your astral temple with the assistance of Andrealphus or the energy of Andrealphus (whichever shows up). When you record how this went in your journal, be sure to record how Andrealphus manifested for you and how your energy meshed with the Daemon's.

Week 65 - Andrealphus - Create a Spell or Ritual

Today, create a spell or ritual (or magical artifact, i.e., talisman) working with Andrealphus for one of the following:

1. Psychic self-defense (an talisman would be great here and you should make one.)
2. To seal a portal.
3. To protect your astral temple.
4. To bring closure to any situation.
5. To dissolve obstacles.

Week 65 - Andrealphus – Rest / Reflect / Plan / Meditate

How did you feel about the astral and mental work with Andrealphus this week? How did you feel about more practical work you may have done? Do you feel better prepared to deal with psychic attacks? Do you feel Andrealphus taught you anything about psychic self-defense? How did you mesh with the Daemon? How did Andrealphus' energy make you feel in the beginning vs late in the week? How did it change?

WEEK 66: CIMEJES

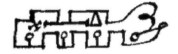

MARQUIS
Color: Violet
Incense: Jasmine
Metal: Silver
Planet: Moon
Element: Earth
Enn: (also Cimeies or Kimaris) – Ayer avage secore Cimejes
Date: January 10 -19

Original Purpose: Invoke to find lost or hidden things or to learn grammar, rhetoric, or logic.

Author's Notes: I have worked with Cimejes successfully for writing success. I've also found this is the Daemon to work with to get help with communication or to open up communication with someone. Cimejes can help job seekers network with one another.

Week 66 - Cimejes - Meditation

For my personal notes on this Daemon, I have listed: Manifestation of intuitions, Daemon of Writers, communication and networking for one's career, and to uncover hidden facts, information, or inspiration via communication. Cimejes is a communication Daemon, so while you're drawing the Daemon's sigil and meditating on Cimejes, consider your own communication skills, not only spoken, but written, and in thought as well (since that's often how we communicate with the unseen).

Week 66 - Cimejes - Freewrite

How can you improve your communication and what doors would this open for you? This could have to do with relationships, career, or even spirit communication. How can you open the line of communication with spirits or other people to manifest your will? How much of your Great Work relies on communication with others, with yourself, or with the spirit world? What is your communication style? Could Cimejes help you with public speaking? Or writing? How?

Week 66 - Cimejes- Dreamwork

Use tonight's dreamwork session to take the sigil with you as you ascend to your astral temple and communicate with Cimejes. As you write up any experiences in your dream journal (or even the words: Nothing happened, or whatever) - let your mind wander freely and feel free to write down whatever comes to mind. Just let yourself go and write out whatever comes through your brain upon waking, no matter how nonsensical or random it may seem.

Week 66 - Cimejes - Invocation/Evocation #1

Today, invoke Cimejes and do one of the following:

1. A divination session. Scrying or even spirit board (properly prepared of course)
2. An automatic writing session. Invite the energy of Cimejes into you, feel the Daemonic spirit within to inspire you - then write. See what comes of it.
3. Consecrate a seal of Cimejes to carry with you to work for the rest of the week with the intent to network and communicate better with co-workers.
4. Do your own thing. If you're a writer, maybe invoke Cimejes and sit your butt down in the chair and do some writing!

Week 66 - Cimejes - Invocation/Evocation #2

Today, invoke Cimejes and repeat yesterday's exercise or choose a new one! Basically - practice communicating.

1. A divination session. Scrying or even spirit board (properly prepared of course)
2. An automatic writing session. Invite the energy of Cimejes into you, feel the Daemonic spirit within to inspire you - then write. See what comes of it.

3. Consecrate a seal of Cimejes to carry with you to work for the rest of the week with the intent to network and communicate better with co-workers.
4. Do your own thing. If you're a writer, maybe invoke Cimejes and sit your butt down in the chair and do some writing!

You can even invoke Cimejes to rehearse a public speaking bit. He'll give you some feedback.

Week 66 - Cimejes - Create a Spell or Ritual

Create a spell, ritual, or magickal artifact for one of the following by working with Cimejes:

1. Talisman for better communication/writing.
2. A spell to open communication (with spirits or people - your choice)
3. To heighten one's intuition.
4. To draw opportunities for networking.

Week 66 - Cimejes- Rest/Reflect/Plan/Meditate

How do you feel about your communication before Cimejes and afterward? What areas do you need to work on? What areas do you excel in? What did Cimejes reveal to you? How was your week with this spirit and would you work with Cimejes again? How does this Daemonic force interact with your physical energy?

WEEK 67: AMDUCIUS

DUKE
Color: Green
Incense: Sandalwood
Metal: Copper
Planet: Venus
Element: Air
Enn: (also Amdusias or Amdusius, Amdukias)–
Denyen valocur avage secore Amdusias
Date: January 20 - 29

Original Purpose: Gives excellent familiars and causes trees to bend to the magician's will.

Author's Notes: Invoke during more aggressive pursuits and execration magicks. Some Daemonolaters believe Amducius, Asmodeus /Asmoday, and Amaymon are the three heads of the three headed Asmodai image from Collin de Plancy's *Dictionnaire Infernal*. Amducius being the more aggressive of the three to be employed during battle and situations requiring an aggressive strategy with military precision.

See the Appendices and the article about the

Asmodai for more insight into Amducius.

Week 67 - Amducius - Meditation

In the Daemonolatry world, Amducius is actually Airy/Fire and is an active, diplomatic force. So, in execration he helps one outwit/outsmart an enemy - or work diplomatically to solve an issue through direct confrontation and diplomacy. This makes him great for people who need a bit of self-confidence, and feeling powerful enough to protect themselves and their ideas verbally. That said, Amducius is a musician's Daemon by drawing attention and visibility to a musician's talent and completed work/projects. But, if you're not musically inclined, you can still work with him to bring strength and confidence into your life and to build up your arsenal against verbal attack from others.

All of this said - as you're focusing/meditating on Amducius today, I want you to draw the sigil into yourself and see if you can activate your own internal Amducius. Your internal power to stand up for yourself. Your internal confidence. Your ability to influence and manifest through diplomacy and carefully thought-out tactics. The desire and passion for personal power over our own lives. Amducius says, "You have the power within you. Own it."

Week 67 - Amducius - Freewrite

In what areas of your life do you feel powerless? How can you take back that power? How much of your power do you give to others by allowing them to manipulate your emotional state? Better yet, who uses your emotional openness to hurt you and why do you allow it? How can you take down detractors, critics, or enemies using diplomacy and tact against them?

Week 67 - Amducius- Dreamwork

Tonight, visualize the sigil of Amducius as you're falling asleep while also visualizing yourself being imbued with an orange glow of strength. Ascend to the astral if you can and use this power to clean up any astral sludge, nastiness, or personal attachments/curses that you've allowed to live in your most sacred space (your mind). What does this exercise manifest for you? Did you dream? Did you sleep better? Were you restless all night? What were your immediate thoughts upon waking?

Week 67 - Amducius - Invocation/Evocation #1

Today, I want you to do your invocation in the morning if possible. Once the energy in the room changes, draw the energy of Amducius into you. Or bless his sigil on a piece of paper, or if you have a sigil set - draw the energy into it — and carry it with you the rest of the day. Make sure you imbue this sigil with strength, confidence, and a no-nonsense, don't fuck with me, attitude.

How did people react to you all day? How did you feel? How did you communicate? Was the Daemon's energy too intense or just right? Did you feel dehydrated, or scatter brained? Or did you feel focused and determined?

Please note - for some people - this may make you more aggressive or even mean. So be careful of this. Especially if you're particularly sensitive to charged sigils (some people are hypersensitive due to mediumship ability).

Week 67 - Amducius - Invocation/Evocation #2

Today, invoke Amducius and think of one thing you'd like to feel more confident about. Now, ascend to the astral and visualize yourself becoming more confident in that area. Visit your astral temple and speak to Amducius about this and see what wisdom he offers.

Be sure to write up all the details in your journal. Remember that you're welcome to insert your own exercise, or do your own thing during each Invocation, even if it's just a meditation with the Daemonic energy. However, I think confidence building exercises with the Daemonic can really help us change the things about ourselves we'd like to change, so at least consider trying one.

Week 67 - Amducius - Create a Spell or Ritual

Today, with the aid of Amducius, create a spell, ritual, or magickal artifact for one of the following:

1. A charm for confidence.
2. A spell or ritual for visibility of your music.
3. A protection spell.
4. A ritual to overcome an enemy (whether person, situation, or habit).

Week 67 - Amducius – Rest / Reflect / Plan / Meditate

What did exploring passion and power teach you this week? How did you relate to Amducius mentally, emotionally, physically, and spiritually? What lessons will you take from this week going forward? Has Amducias earned a spot in your personal pantheon?

WEEK 68: BELIAL

KING
Color: Yellow
Incense: Frankincense
Metal: Gold
Planet: Sun
Element: Fire (Earth)
Enn: Lirach Tasa Vefa Wehlc Belial
Date: January 30 – February 8

Original Purpose: Distributes titles and can make friends and enemies favor your position. He gives familiars. The magician must give offerings, sacrifices, and gifts if he wants Belial to be truthful.

Author's Notes: In the Dukanté hierarchy, Belial is seen as the representative Daemonic force of Earth. In this aspect, he is the destructive Earth force. This makes invoking this aspect apt for execrations and necromancy not to mention business endeavors that require aggressive measures.

Week 68 - Belial - Meditation

As you're drawing Belial's sigil today, I want you to think of ACTIVE manifesting. Some Earth elemental Daemons are passive, but because Belial can fall in either Earth (Dukanté) or Fire (Goetia) (which is why he's celebrated during the Winter Solstice - which is an Earthy Fire Festival) he is an active force. Visualize the sigil moving and pushing out its own energy. Feel that energy within yourself. You are an active force for manifestation. Belial, in this sense, makes an incredible Malkuth on the tree of life.

Week 68 - Belial - Freewrite

Today, write about what you can manifest. What can you destroy that no longer serves? What active manifestations could you use right now? What is at a stalemate that could use some movement? Maybe just a little shove in the right direction. Write about your preconceived notions about Belial. Since this is a Daemon many people have worked with, as Belial tends to be high in the popularity department, what are your expectations based on previous work you've done?

Week 68 - Belial - Dreamwork

Tonight, as you're drifting off to sleep with the sigil clear in your mind, I'd like you to take with you the intention to speak with Belial about where you need to focus your energy. Ask the Daemon to send you a dream giving you some guidance in this area.

As soon as you awake, write down any immediate thoughts, memories of dreams, or ideas that came to you, even if it seems nonsensical. I once dreamed I hugged a priest and he farted - the subtext of the dream being that no one is perfect or above reproach.

Everyone farts. So, when you have weird dreams, realize there's always a subtext or message in them, even if that message has a non-metaphysical meaning.

Week 68 - Belial - Invocation/Evocation #1

Today I want you to invoke Belial with the intent to draw opportunities for wealth, more money, and abundance (even if that is emotional abundance or an abundance of friends) to you. You can simply do a meditative visualization or burn a green or brown candle to symbolize the opportunities coming to you, or you can do a simple request ritual where you write out what you want. Sign it. Draw the Daemon's sigil on it. Put a drop of blood on it (if you're not scared) and then burn it in the offering bowl. I guarantee Belial will draw opportunities to you - even if those opportunities are for self-improvement to help you make the changes you need to make in order to manifest more abundance in your life. Remember that Daemons are teachers. They often bring us lessons more than just dropping things in our lap, and even when they do drop things in our laps, sometimes there's still a lesson attached.

Week 68 - Belial - Invocation/Evocation #2

For today's invocation - once you feel the energy of the room change, I want you to draw the active flowing Fire/Earth manifesting energy of Belial into you. Then go about your day. Do it in the morning to see if your energy level has improved.
As applies when working with any Fire Daemon - be sure to stay well hydrated. Leave room in your journal to write how your day went. Was your energy improved? Did you feel more focused? Did any opportunities manifest? Were you gifted something, or did you end up getting an unexpected gift or payment? Did you have especially positive and productive interactions with others?

Week 68 - Belial - Create a Spell or Ritual

Create a spell, ritual, or magickal artifact in the name of Belial - or with the aid of Belial - for one of the following:

1. An energy drawing talisman to help you stay on track and work toward manifesting your goals.
2. A draw opportunity spell/ritual.
3. A money drawing ritual.
4. A manifestation ritual. To manifest anything.

Week 68 - Belial - Rest/Reflect/Plan/Meditate

How was this week with Belial? If you've worked with Belial before, how did this week differ? How did your personal energy meld with Belial's? What opportunities or things manifested for you this week? Did you feel things in your life moving forward? Did stagnated areas improve? Write all of this down in your journal and leave a little space just in case you want to come back later and add to it.

WEEK 69: DECARABIA

MARQUIS
Color: Violet
Incense: Jasmine
Metal: Silver
Planet: Moon
Element: Air
Enn: Hoesta noc ra Decarabia secore
Date: February 9 - 18

Original Purpose: Helps the magician discover the virtues of birds and stones.

Author's Notes: To uncover or help hide deceptions. Also seek Decarabia to free oneself of obstacles or situations holding you back. Decarabia can help the magician rise above the petty and the ego even if only for a short time.

Week 69 - Decarabia - Meditation

Go into today's meditation with the intention to be open and to learn something new this week. Draw the sigil, think of the Daemon, and think about uncovering hidden truth. Open yourself and your mind up to a new experience. Decarabia is expansive and the magicians who work with him tend to broaden their minds and come to see things that others do not. This may also be a good time to do a visualization of you rising above your problems and seeing them for what they actually are.

Week 69 - Decarabia - Freewrite

What obstacles do you need to remove right now? What influences do you need? Who do you need to get on your side? In what situations would it benefit you to rise above your initial emotional reaction for a fresh perspective? What information do you need to uncover?

Week 69 - Decarabia- Dreamwork

Tonight, as you're falling asleep, thinking of Dcarabia, visualize yourself separating from your ego so that you become two separate people. What does this visualization look like? What dreams does it spark? What initial thoughts as you awaken? Do you remember talking to anyone in your dreams?

Week 69 - Decarabia - Invocation/Evocation #1

Today, invoke Decarabia with the intent to destroy all obstacles. Once you feel the Daemon's presence in the ritual space, visualize that Daemonic energy growing and growing, filling the room, filling your town or city. Filling your state or country, then the continent. Then the world - obliterating ALL obstacles. Okay, so you don't have to go as far as the whole world but grow Decarabia's energy big enough to just destroy the obstacles in YOUR path. Then give it a week and see what happens. Be sure to note how a ritual like this made you feel mentally. Did it clear out some mental clutter or worry? Remember that sometimes our thoughts are our own obstacles. Leave space to come back a week from now to fill in what manifested from this.

Week 69 - Decarabia - Invocation/Evocation #2

Today, invoke Decarabia until the vibration in the room changes, then do one of the following:

1. A request ritual to uncover a deception.
2. A meditation to rise above the ego. (For perspective)
3. A communication/divination session.

Remember that you can use whatever method of invocation/evocation you wish to use. What's important here is what you're doing is working and drawing the Daemonic force to you.

If, for any reason, you're struggling to connect, remember to balance yourself, go back to the breath, focus, clean your own energy, and ask yourself what's going on in your life (mundane life) that is holding you back. Oftentimes an inability to connect is due to a busy mundane life, or outright stress from the mundane world. You're not alone. This is normal. If that's the case, just do some gentle meditation sessions instead of the magickal work until you are able to "feel" the Daemonic again.

Week 69 - Decarabia - Create a Spell or Ritual

Today, create a spell or ritual with the assistance of Decarabia for one of the following:

1. To destroy obstacles.
2. To glamor someone else.
3. To uncover what is hidden.

Week 69 - Decarabia – Rest / Reflect / Plan /Meditate

What did you learn about your own ego this week? Your obstacles? Your mental clutter? Did Decarabia help you influence or glamor someone? Were you drawn to more natural forms of magick? (i.e., stones, herbs, etc.) Were you able to remove some things holding you back? How do you and Decarabia work together? Chalk and cheese? Peanut Butter and Jelly?

WEEK 70: SEERE

PRINCE
Color: Blue
Incense: Cedar
Metal: Tin
Planet: Jupiter
Element: Air (Fire)
Enn: (also Sear or Seir)- Jeden et Renich Seere tu tasa
Date: February 19 - 28

Original Purpose: Will bring certain situations to pass and to help you modify your life. He can help find thieves and lead you to treasure. The Goetia says he's good-natured.

Author's Notes: To have a clear perception of any situation or person unfettered by emotional upset or preconceived notions. I also found Seere to be good natured.

Week 70 - Seere - Meditation

The name Seere itself suggests some kind of divination, doesn't it? Not surprisingly, Seere is anything but a divination Daemon. Can Seere lead you to gnosis and give you clear perception? Absolutely. Can Seere uncover thieves and protect your home from them? Also yes. Can Seere make things go your way and bring you opportunities to travel? You bet your boots Seere can. But help you learn to scry? Not necessarily one of Seere's strongest talents. As you draw Seere's seal today and you're thinking of the Daemon and its attributes, I want you to keep an open mind just to see if Seere inspires you to consider things you may not have considered.

Week 70 - Seere - Freewrite

Today, write about what things need to go your way this week. Write about your favorite trip with loved ones or friends. Write about your personal spiritual journey and what you hope to get from your spiritual practice overall. It never hurts to write about these things because magickal journals are part mundane, part spiritual, but mostly self-discovery and understanding. They become records of your innermost thoughts and feelings. They reveal the shadow work we need to do.

Week 70 - Seere - Dreamwork

Go into sleep tonight with the seal beneath your

mattress or pillow and with the intent to have Seere lead you to gnosis. What revelations will the Daemon bring? Write down anything you remember from your dreams, or any thoughts you have upon waking no matter how ridiculous or even nonsensical it seems. Sometimes we may not know at the time what the dream or our waking thoughts are telling us until we've had some time and space and are looking back in reflection. I know - you're probably thinking "A lot of good it does me now" but trust me — it will be revelatory at some point.

Week 70 - Seere - Invocation/Evocation #1

Today, invoke Seere and do one of the following:

1. Create a protection talisman to carry with you.
2. Do a request ritual to ask that things go your way or to draw opportunities for travel.
3. Draw the Daemonic force into you for clear perception.
4. Do a divination or ascension session to speak with the Daemon about any matter.

Or do whatever works for you today.

Week 70 - Seere - Invocation/Evocation #2

Today, invoke Seere and choose something

different (or the same) from the list:

1. Create a protective talisman to carry with you.
2. Do a request ritual to ask that things go your way or to draw opportunities for travel.
3. Draw the Daemonic force into you for clear perception.
4. Do a divination or ascension session to speak with the Daemon about any matter.

Or do whatever works for you today. Remember that you get to decide what you have the time and energy for each day.

Week 70 - Seere - Create a Spell or Ritual

A sigil of Seere hung at the entrance of a home wards thieves goes the old saying in a friend's home. All her kids have the sigil of Seere over their doors, she has one over hers, and her mother has one over hers. One year, she gave me one, and it hung over my door for years until the hanger broke off and it fell to the floor and shattered. I have yet to find someone who makes ceramic sigils so I could replace it.

I think this week it would be fun to make your own seal of Seere to place over your front door, or somewhere near the entrance of your home. Make it out of clay, wood, metal, or do a painting or whatever craft you feel comfortable working in. You could even just draw it out, or print it and color it, and put it in a frame and hang it. But not before imbuing the seal with the intent of protecting your home against theft.

Week 70 - Seere - Rest/Reflect/Plan/Meditate

Did Seere provide any pivotal gnosis this week? Did you create the home protection sigil and hang it in your home? If so, how does your home feel now as opposed to before you placed the seal? Did any opportunities for travel present themselves? Do you feel your perception of a situation or person is clearer now? What went in your favor this week? Do you feel Seere helped with that? How do you feel about Seere overall? Is this a Daemonic force you'd work with again? What physical/emotional responses did this Daemon evoke within you?

WEEK 71: DANTALION

DUKE
Color: Green
Incense: Sandalwood
Metal: Copper
Planet: Venus
Element: Water
Enn: Avage ayer Dantalion on ca
Date: March 1 –10

Original Purpose: Teaches all arts and sciences and has the ability to show you the thoughts of others and to sway the thoughts of others. She can also cause love.

Author's Notes: Helps one relate with others on an emotional level. Teaches emotional intelligence and heightens empathy for others.

Week 71 - Dantalion - Meditation

Fair warning that this week, we're going to laser focus on our thought patterns and the shadow work required to really get into our own heads for the sake of self-healing and mental well-being. Or perhaps you're going to focus on your relationships and draw new friends or lovers to you. You can also choose to use this week to bring closure to something that needs it, or to increase your empathy if you have a reason for that. While you're drawing your sigil of Dantalion today and just meditating on the Daemonic force that is Dantalion, think about these things and make a choice about what you would like to focus on.

Week 71 - Dantalion - Freewrite

Today, write about the area you've decided to focus on for the week. Are you going to try to break a bad habit? Are you going to focus on strengthening or building relationships? If so, why did you choose what you chose? If you don't feel drawn to Dantalion or any of Dantalion's purposes at all (it happens) write about that. What preconceived notions do you have about this week? What depth of practice do you have time for this week? Will you only be meditating on the Daemon? If so, why? Bare your soul to your journal. No one else has to see it. You can even burn it at some point in the future if you see fit.

Week 71 - Dantalion- Dreamwork

Tonight, as you're drifting off to sleep, I want you to focus on some emotional trauma you want to heal. Take Dantalion's enn and sigil into sleep with you. We all have emotional trauma we're dealing with on some level. Or we've dealt with it but may still suffer some triggers from it years later.

How was your quality of sleep last night? Did you have any dreams? Did you wake up with any thoughts on how to better offer yourself self-care to help you heal more deeply?

You're also welcome to take whatever intent you wish into the dream. Remember that each days' exercises are just suggestions. You can modify or change them based on what YOU need.

Week 71 - Dantalion - Invocation/Evocation #1

Today, invoke Dantalion and do a scrying ritual with the Daemon. For those of you who are hardcore traditionalists, you are welcome to do a full-blown goetic ritual for this. For others, make the ritual as simple or as elaborate as you wish. It doesn't need to be elaborate to be effective.

Week 71 - Dantalion - Invocation/Evocation #2

Today, invoke Dantalion - and do a request ritual (see *The Complete Book of Demonolatry* for a basic request ritual structure) asking the Daemon to lend their energy to one of the following areas:

1. To help you change a thought pattern holding you

back.
2. To draw friends/lovers
3. To bring closure to a situation or relationship that no longer serves you.
4. To heal mental/emotional trauma.
5. To heighten empathy and bring you emotional intelligence.

Week 71 - Dantalion - Create a Spell or Ritual

Instead of doing a spell or ritual this time, why not create some kind of talisman to draw:

1. Friends and lovers.
2. Mental well-being.
3. Empathy.

Of course, you're always welcome to create spells or rituals for any of the above, too. This is your creation ritual with Dantalion. What does he inspire you to create today?

Week 71 - Dantalion – Rest / Reflect / Plan / Meditate

Did you find Dantalion's energy comforting? Calming? Do you feel movement or have experiences in the areas of life you worked with Dantalion this week? Does the Daemon make you feel hot? Cold? Energized? Tired? Do you feel dehydrated or hungry after working with them? Do you crave certain foods/drinks? These are the types of things you should note when working with any Daemonic force. It will help you identify any patterns. I once knew a woman who, after working with Dantalion, she had the urge to drink chamomile tea and watch Hallmark movies. Your experience will be your own.

WEEK 72: ANDROMALIUS

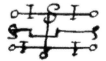

EARL
Color: Red
Incense: Dragon's Blood
Metal: Copper or Silver
Planet: Mars
Element: Fire
Enn: Tasa fubin Andromalius on ca
Date: March 11 -20

Original Purpose: To find thieves and stolen goods, invoke Andromalius. He can also help uncover plots against the magician and punish those involved. He discovers hidden treasures.

Author's Notes: Andromalius works well for execration and protection. Invoke him as a ward in your home to protect against theft or harm to you by other people. Wear his lamen when going out alone or going to dangerous places.

Week 72 - Andromalius - Meditation

While you can work with Andromalius for protection this week if this Daemon feels more in sync with your energy than previous protection Daemons. However, since we worked with Seere for home protection last week (unless you need further protection from physical and mental harm/abuse), let's consider working with Andromalius for execration, and/or good judgement (about other people) this week. As you're doing your meditation on Andromalius today, I want to you relax and think of a time when you poorly judged a situation or person and ended up getting burned.

Week 72 - Andromalius - Freewrite

Today we're going to continue the meditation from yesterday in the freewrite and write about what happened when poor judgment burned you. How long ago did it happen? Did you learn from it? What did you learn? Have you avoided similar situations since? Do you feel you have good judgment? You're also welcome to write about people who have wronged you just to get it out of your system. While you're welcome to do execration magick this week, I don't want to focus on that. I would rather we focus on strengthening our judgment about others and situations, and letting the Daemonic Divine do the judging and punishing. Remember that most people who deserve a Daemonic bitch-slap will likely get what they deserve, because nasty people bring misfortune on themselves and the Daemonic protect their own (unless they think you need a smack-down/lesson.)

Week 72 - Andromalius - Dreamwork

In today's dreamwork, just take the seal of the Daemon with you into the dream and let whatever comes of it, come of it. Does the Daemon send you any imagery in your dreams tonight? Do you wake up feeling tired or refreshed? What thoughts manifest immediately upon waking?

Week 72 - Andromalius - Invocation/Evocation #1

Today, invoke Andromalius and do a scrying ritual with the Daemon. For those of you who are hardcore traditionalists, you are welcome to do a full-blown goetic ritual for this. For others, make the ritual as simple or as elaborate as you wish. It doesn't need to be elaborate to be effective.

Week 72 - Andromalius - Invocation/Evocation #2

Repeat the scrying ritual today, but this time ask the Daemon to reveal any people you should be wary of, and what should be done to keep yourself safe. You can also do automatic writing, spirit board sessions (with prepared boards only), etc.

Week 72 - Andromalius - Create a Spell or Ritual

Today, create a spell or ritual with Andromalius for one of the following:

1. A curse.
2. To reveal who has wronged you.
3. To draw good judgment on people or situations.
4. For warding/protection.

Week 72 - Andromalius – Rest / Reflect / Plan / Meditate

What are your thoughts on your work with Andromalius this week? Did you feel safe in the Daemon's presence? Suffocated? Light? What words would you use to describe the Daemon's energy? Did you find the Daemon intimidating or stand-offish? Sometimes we feel that way with spirits we don't really meld well with initially. Sometimes it requires us to adjust our vibration before working with a particular spirit. The more you can note how a Daemonic force affects you, the more you can adjust or temper that energy to make the Daemon more comfortable to work with. As above, so below.

A Note About the Elements

In the western traditions, there are five elements. Earth, Air, Fire, Water, and Spirit. And almost EVERY magickal tool and component, and even every spirit you work with will have an element associated with it. Even you have an elemental alignment based on your astrological makeup at your time of birth. This is also why elemental balancing is an energy work exercise taught to neophyte Daemonolaters as a way of balancing and grounding oneself.

As you've probably guessed - each element has a basic meaning behind it. So, when you see an elemental correspondence, by knowing its meaning, you can get a general idea of what you're looking at.

Each Daemonic force also has an element associated with it, and it can give us some idea as to which directional point to invoke that particular spirit from.

ABOUT ELEMENTAL DIRECTIONS AND
CONFLICTING INFORMATION ACROSS
DIFFERENT SYSTEMS:

Agrippa

Please note that in Agrippa the elements fall in
these particular directions, and some say this
makes the most sense based on the zodiac and
wheel of the year. Earth - South, Air - West, Fire -
East, and Water - North. In instances like this, like
many magickal correspondences, it's subjective.
While you can choose the directions that make the
most sense to you, it's good to know that different
correspondence systems exist. You can read the
reasoning behind Agrippa's choices by reading his
Books of Occult Philosophy. If you agree with it, feel
free to use the above directional correspondences.

Western Witchcraft

Many Daemonolaters tend to use a more traditional
craft elemental set-up because there is a lot of folk
magick - traditional witchcraft influences a lot of
traditional Daemonolatry. North (or West) - Earth,
East - Air, South - Fire, and West (or North) - Water.

Use what makes the most sense to you, and the
magick you're working, because your
correspondences need to work with your way of
thinking in order for you to establish clear intent,

which is one of the most important ingredients in any magickal work (including invocation).

It's probably important to understand that even in the Water-West and Earth-North model, that Water and Earth can change places.

	Witchcraft	Agrippa
EARTH	North or West	South
AIR	East	West
FIRE	South	East
WATER	West or North	North

Water North - Water West?

This can be super confusing to those who may just be starting out. So, the first thing is that Water and Earth trade places in different traditions. Some systems, like the Khemetic system, put Water North. If you're working alchemically or within certain ceremonial traditions, it makes more sense to put Water North. If you practice traditional craft or certain forms of Western ceremonial magick, however, Water is often put toward the west.

In my humble opinion though — it really depends on the operation. IF you're looking to stabilize emotions, strengthen wisdom, or manifest greater clarity through divination, or to heighten your intuition — Water North because it's closer to Air, thus affecting mental acuity. If you're looking to spark creativity, explore your passions, or destroy someone else – Water west to heighten emotion and infuse it with Fire.

So, in this sense, you can look at the elements as Air and Fire being "fixed elements" and Earth and Water as being "mutable elements" within a magickal circle with an elemental construct.

Ultimately – if you haven't tried Earth toward the West and Water to the North — try it. Decide which one you like better. I've noticed everyone has their preference. I can go either way.

Just as an aside here, when you're working with the Fire Aspect of Belial, it makes sense to put Earth West. IF you're working with the Cold/Dry Earth aspect of Belial, it makes sense to put Earth North.

The Goetia Elementals

People often forget that the Goetia actually includes 76 spirits because you can't forget the four Elemental Kings. And you'll find in different renditions of the MS, there are different names. For King of the East - Uriens or Oriens, sometimes it's listed as Amaymon. For King of the South - We find Amaymon or Corson. For King of the West -

Paymon or Goap. And finally, King of the North is Egyn or Zimimar.

I would work with Amaymon (Fire), Corson (Earth), Goap (Air), and Egyn (Water) if you're working with the Agrippa elemental construct.

I would work with Oriens/Uriens (Air), Amaymon (Fire), Paymon (Water), and Zimimar (Earth) if you tend toward a more modern Witchcraft elemental construct.

Or do your own thing if something else makes more sense to you. The above are merely suggestions, not gospel.

Which is why I'll be giving you some options for each set of spirits. I know some people need more direction than this, but there's a reason this is a more advanced class/book — because you should already have enough experience that you don't need hand holding and you can direct yourself and your own spiritual growth based on what you know about you and what works FOR YOU. There are no one-true-ways in spirituality/magick since it's very subjective to the individual experiencing it.

Some Generalized Meanings of each Element:

EARTH: Manifestation, motherhood, stability, abundance, fertility, foundation, birth, the physical/mundane world.

AIR: Communication, thought, mental creativity, decision making, focus, education/learning, the mental world.

FIRE: Energy, love, lust, motivation, the creative muse, warmth and safety, self-defense, and the divine spark.

WATER: Intuition, healing, empathy, emotional intelligence, nurturing, and the psychic world

Elemental Balancing Ritual

Sit comfortably in a quiet place where you won't be disturbed. During the first part of this ritual, you will visualize removing all of your "used" or "spent" elements from you.

Do this by imagining you are holding a box. Into this box you put all of your elements, one at a time, and then throw the box away from you. You may have to fill the box with each element more than once.

Imagine Earth as soil and leaves - these are the burdens in life you no longer need. So, pull them from yourself and toss them into this box. Imagine Air as black smoke. You're putting all your worries and mental frustrations into the box via the black smoke of negativity that you're purging from your body. Visualize Fire as dying embers you are pulling from yourself (lethargy, procrastination, boredom, and dullness), and Water being specific to throw in emotions no longer serving you, especially anger, fear, worry, anxiety. Put all this bullshit into the boxes and throw them away from you, visualizing these old, used up elements being thrown out. Once you have removed all your elements and feel a bit tired and emotionally drained - and you will be able to tell because you will feel it -- you can begin replenishing that which you have freed yourself of.

Imagine refilling the box with "fresh" elements. Fill your Earth box with growing green things and rich soil - stability and strength and manifestation. Fill your Air box with new ideas, clear thoughts, and focus. Fill your Fire box with fresh flames dancing around - motivation, energy, and vitality. And fill your Water box with fresh water - hopefulness, happiness, and contentment. Only fill the box once with each element. As you fill each box, pull it into your torso, visualizing your aura changing color to represent that element.

When this is done correctly you will feel invigorated and energetic. You will be doing this exercise at least once a week during your work with the elemental kings.

WEEK 73: King of the East - Uriens or Amaymon

Jen da Uriens elat
Elan Reya Amaymon

IF EAST IS YOUR AIR
Renich Tasa Uberaca Biasa Icar [Daemonic force]

IF EAST IS YOUR FIRE
Ganic Tasa Fubin [Daemonic Force]

Week 73 - Uriens or Amaymon - Meditation

Face EAST and perform an elemental balancing ritual, paying special focus to the element you associate with the EAST.

Week 73 - Uriens or Amaymon - Freewrite

Write down what the element you associate with this direction means to you. For example: if East is your Air - what do you associate with Air? Which spirits feel particularly Airy for you? Do you associate more with Uriens or Amaymon? How does this element make you feel?

Week 73 - Uriens or Amaymon - Dreamwork

Visualize yourself immersed in the element you associate with the EAST tonight. If it's Air, take deep breaths. If it's Fire, imagine yourself warm and fueled with passion. What comes of this sleep? How do you feel about this particular element and direction?

Week 73 - Uriens or Amaymon - Invocation/Evocation #1

Invoke the appropriate spirit and just sit in its presence. If you associate this direction with Air, focus on your breath. If you associate this direction with Fire, scry with a candle flame. What comes of it?

Week 73 - Uriens or Amaymon -

Invocation/Evocation #2

Perform the same invocation today or do whatever you wish. Like, if you associate East with Fire, maybe use this invocation to draw energy to yourself. Or to give you motivation.

Week 73 - Uriens or Amaymon - Create a Spell or Ritual

Create a spell or ritual consistent with the meanings behind the element you associate with this direction.

Week 73 - Uriens or Amaymon - Rest/Reflect/Plan/Meditate

How do you feel about this particular element and direction and spirit associated with it? Do you feel balanced or imbalanced at the end of this week? How so?

WEEK 74: King of the South - Amaymon or Corson

Week 74 - King of the South - Amaymon or Corson

Elan Reya Amaymon
Ana tasa Corson nanay

IF SOUTH IS YOUR FIRE
Ganic Tasa Fubin [Daemonic Force]

IF SOUTH IS YOUR EARTH
Lirach Tasa Vefa Wehlcc [Daemonic Force]

Week 74 - Amaymon or Corson - Meditation

Face SOUTH and perform an elemental balancing ritual, paying special focus to the element you associate with the SOUTH.

Week 74 - Amaymon or Corson - Freewrite

Write down what the element you associate with this direction means to you. For example: if South is your Fire - what do you associate with Fire? Which spirits feel particularly fiery for you? Do you connect more with Amaymon or Corson? How does this element make you feel?

Week 74 - Amaymon or Corson - Dreamwork

Visualize yourself immersed in the element you associate with the SOUTH tonight. If it's Fire, imagine yourself warm and fueled with passion. If it's Earth, visualize yourself growing roots into the ground. What comes of this sleep? How do you feel about this particular element and direction?

Week 74 - Amaymon or Corson - Invocation/Evocation #1

Invoke the appropriate (to you) spirit and just sit in its presence. If you associate this direction with Fire, focus on a candle flame. If you associate this direction with Earth, scry with a crystal. What comes of it?

Week 74 - Amaymon or Corson - Invocation/Evocation #2

Perform the same invocation today or do whatever you wish. Like, if you associate South with Fire, maybe use this invocation to draw energy to yourself. Or to give you motivation. If Earth, use it to ground yourself or build firm foundation.

Week 74 - Amaymon or Corson - Create a Spell or Ritual

Create a spell or ritual consistent with the meanings behind the element you associate with this direction.

Week 74 - Amaymon or Corson - Rest/Reflect/Plan/Meditate

How do you feel about this particular element and direction and spirit associated with it? Do you feel balanced or imbalanced at the end of this week? How so?

WEEK 75: King of the West - Paymon or Gaap

Linan tasa jedan Paimon.
Anana avac Gaap

IF WEST IS YOUR WATER
Jedan Tasa Hoet Naca [Daemonic Force]

IF WEST IS YOUR EARTH
Lirach Tasa Vefa Wehlcc [Daemonic Force]

IF WEST IS YOUR AIR
Renich Tasa Uberaca Biasa Icar [Daemonic force]

Week 75 - Paymon or Gaap - Meditation

Face WEST and perform an elemental balancing ritual, paying special focus to the element you associate with the WEST.

Week 75 - Paymon or Gaap - Freewrite

Write down what the element you associate with this direction means to you. For example: if West is your Water - what do you associate with Water? Which spirits feel particularly Watery for you? Do you associate more with Paymon or Gaap? How does this element make you feel?

Week 75 - Paymon or Gaap - Dreamwork

Visualize yourself immersed in the element you associate with the WEST tonight. If it's Water, be mindful of your feelings. If it's Air, try to focus on a trail of incense smoke or focus on the breath. If it's Earth, ground yourself with roots going through the bed into the ground. What comes of this sleep? How do you feel about this particular element and direction?

Week 75 - Paymon or Gaap - Invocation/Evocation #1

Invoke the spirit you associate with the West and just sit in its presence. If you associate this direction with Water, focus on calming the emotions. Scry in a bowl of water, or in incense smoke, or in a crystal. What comes of it?

Week 75 - Paymon or Gaap - Invocation/Evocation #2

Perform the same invocation today or do whatever you wish. Like, if you associate West with Earth, maybe use this invocation to ground any excess energy.

Week 75 - Paymon or Gaap - Create a Spell or Ritual

Create a spell or ritual consistent with the meanings behind the element you associate with this direction.

Week 75 - Paymon or Gaap - Rest/Reflect/Plan/Meditate

How do you feel about this particular element and direction and spirit associated with it? Do you feel balanced or imbalanced at the end of this week? How so?

WEEK 76: King of the North - Egyn or Zimimar (also Zimimay)

Elat anan Egyn
Renin Zimimar et élan

IF NORTH IS YOUR EARTH
Lirach Tasa Vefa Wehlcc [Daemonic Force]

IF NORTH IS YOUR WATER
Jedan Tasa Hoet Naca [Daemonic Force]

Week 76 - Egyn or Zimimar - Meditation

Face NORTH and perform an elemental balancing ritual, paying special focus to the element you associate with the NORTH.

Week 76 - Egyn or Zimimar- Freewrite

Write down what the element you associate with this direction means to you. For example: if North is your Water - what do you associate with Water? Which spirits feel particularly Watery for you? Do you associate more with Egyn or Zimimar? How does this element make you feel?

Week 76 - Egyn or Zimimar - Dreamwork

Visualize yourself immersed in the element you associate with the NORTH tonight. If it's Water, take time to calm yourself and be aware of how you're feeling. If it's Earth, imagine yourself being grounded, or even manifesting something. What comes of this sleep? How do you feel about this particular element and direction?

Week 76 - Egyn or Zimimar - Invocation/Evocation #1

Invoke the spirit you're most comfortable with and just sit in its presence. If you associate this direction with Earth, focus on feeling heavy and tethered to the ground. Being part of everything. Become aware of the physical body. If you associate this direction with Water, scry in a bowl of water. What comes of it?

Week 76 - Egyn or Zimimar - Invocation/Evocation #2

Perform the same invocation today or do whatever you wish. Like, if you associate the north with Water, maybe use this invocation consecrate tools, or for healing. For Earth, focus on manifesting.

Week 76 - Egyn or Zimimar - Create a Spell or Ritual

Create a spell or ritual consistent with the meanings behind the element you associate with this direction.

Week 76 - Egyn or Zimimar - Rest/Reflect/Plan/Meditate

How do you feel about this particular element and direction and spirit associated with it? Do you feel balanced or imbalanced at the end of this week? How so?

Course Reflection

Course Reflection

After such an intense work, I think it's always wise to give yourself one to four weeks for reflection on your Goetia Immersion experience. I know it sounds pretentious to call it an *experience,* but those who have made it through the full course will tell you that's exactly what it is. Take a few days to reflect, in your journal, on what the experience meant to you. Go back through your journals for the last year and a half (or the length of time you took to go through the immersion) and fill in any blanks or add additional observations you may have missed. Sometimes hindsight is 20/20 and without review and reflection, we can't see the full scope of what we've just been through.

You may see growth from the beginning of your journal entries to the end. You will more readily see the changes you've gone through in the last year and a half upon reflection. Small changes you may not have noticed initially because they didn't feel like big things. Changes in perception, or in how you approach things, or even how you think of magick or the Daemonic in general.

Ask yourself a few questions:

1. What did this experience teach me?
2. Which Daemons really stick out now that it's over with.
3. How have I changed since beginning this immersion?
4. How have I stayed the same since beginning this immersion?
5. What has changed in my life for the better?
6. What has changed in my life for the worse?
7. Has my path work undergone a complete overhaul?
8. A year and a half ago - am I where I thought I would be now?
9. What is my biggest takeaway about my magickal practice from this experience?
10. Do I feel more confident as a magician?

Add your own questions! This was YOUR pathworking experience with the Goetic spirits. No one can define this experience for you. No one except you can validate it. This was about you and your relationship with the Daemonic Divine. There was no middleman required. This course, and all the exercises herein, were just a general guide to keep you going. To give you ideas and inspiration. Ultimately — did you emerge from this experience changed? If yes, the immersion did its job. If not, really ask yourself why that was. Oftentimes, what we gain from an experience directly correlates to the effort we put forth.

I recommend waiting awhile before repeating the immersion just so you can tie up any loose ends from all the work you did in the past year and a half. This can take up to a decade. (There's a reason I teach this course once every 7-10 years - it's a lot to work through.)

But congratulations - you did it! I'm proud of you. Not everyone has worked through all 72 Goetic spirits as a method of pathworking/shadow work. Now go forth and manifest your Great Work! You are a divine spark! You are a magician — go forth and CREATE!

Appendices

Asmodai: An Unholy Trinity
S. Connolly

Asmodeus from Collin DePlancy's Dictionnaire Infernal

It is said Asmodai derives from the Avestan phrase *aēšma-daēva, meaning "wrath spirit", or as I prefer to say, "Spirit of wrath". As Asmodeus, he is the Daemon from Talmudic legends, the grand antagonist in the building of the Temple of Solomon, one of the seven Crown Princes of Hell who presides over lust. Allegedly he is a King of Nine Hells in the writings of Renaissance clergymen. In Goetia he is King Asmoday, ruling over legions of Daemonic soldiers. In Goetia he is also Amducius/Amducias, a spirit of musicians and tempests. The name of Asmodeus, like many Daemons, has numerous variants and spellings.

Notice in all of these descriptions that these three Daemonic forces possess the same underlying currents – desire and passion. Desire is the *want*, whereas passion is *the drive* to obtain the *want*.

In Daemonolatry, this is where a different perspective comes into play. We remove all the mythology and look at what these Daemons embody. As it was explained to me during my apprenticeship, three headed, the Asmodai (desires/passions) are Asmoday, Asmodeus, and Amducias. Three aspects of a similar motivating force - each of which is passionate in its own right. Perhaps even wrathful if you could harness the passion behind wrath over the negativity. Passion itself is not negative or positive, it simply is. Asmodeus is sexual desire and passion. Amducias is desire and passion for vengeance/wrath, and perhaps even power. Asmoday is desire and passion for wealth and success.

Asmodai encourages us to explore our desires and find the source of them. To obtain that which we desire. He/it (they) encourages us in our momentum forward toward our goals and that exploration of all of those things we desire. Desire motivates passion. Desire can also be crippling, manifesting jealousy or addiction. Desire drives us to work hard, mate, and build empires. It can also drive us to war. It can help us find companionship or cause us to be forever alone jumping from lover to lover. Without desire, what are we? We are barren. So, in that sense, the Daemonic Asmodai forces enrich us and are a path to abundance.

The following ritual meditation will not only help the practitioner connect with the Asmodai current, but also connect with any individual Daemonic force within this most unholy trinity.

Items Need:

Three red candles inscribed with the following:

Cupiditas Asmodai

Anoint the candles with cinnamon and benzoin macerated in grape seed oil.

Now draw the seals upon parchment. You can use personalized or variant seals of these Daemons. For reference, the seals of the three are thus:

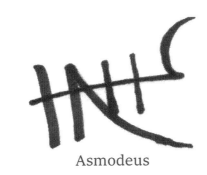

Asmodeus

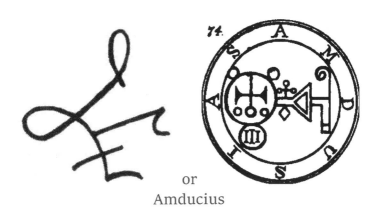

or
Amducius

Asmoday

This ritual is going to be set up in a triangle/pyramid construct. Basically, what you'll do here is place one candle over each of the seals in a triangle large enough for you to sit in. The directional placement can be subjective here. I prefer Amducias Southeast, Asmoday North, and Asmodeus Southwest if I'm using the elemental configuration North/Earth, East/Air, South/Fire, and West/Water. If I am putting Water North and Earth West, I will put Asmodeus in the South, Asmoday Northwest and Amducias Northeast. Go with your inspiration and personal associations here. Don't forget to consider alchemical combinations.

Prepare yourself by bathing, drinking a glass of water, and anointing your third eye with flying ointment or the infusion of cinnamon and benzoin. *Please be careful and test ALL anointing oils on your leg to make sure you won't have an allergic reaction to it first (before anointing your third eye with anything).*

Sit within the triangle nude (or wearing white robes or clothing if you must be clothed), face the south quadrant of the room, and close your eyes. Take a deep breath. Ground and center yourself.

Next, intone the following Enns until your body is vibrating with their essence:

Asmodeus - *Ayer avage Aloren Asmodeus aken*
Amducius/Amdusias - *Denyen valocur avage secore Amdusias*
Asmoday - *Ayer avage Aloren Asmoday aken*

(A Note About Enns: My theory is they're called enns from the alchemical term ens (entia plural). The ens is the influence or principle that affects us. The essence of something. So essentially, the enns (entia) or enn (en) of a Daemon is basically a way to call upon the essence of that Daemonic force. Oftentimes, in communication with a Daemonic force, a magician will receive variant enns attuned to their personal connection to that Daemon, making them most useful to the magician who received them. So, if you find yourself compelled to modify the above enns, just go with it and see what happens. Don't forget to write it down.)

Now, when working with Asmodeus, some people report feeling the urge to masturbate during ritual. If this happens it's perfectly normal and the magus should do so if the mood strikes. That exploding release of energy during orgasm can be rather satisfying in a connection ritual like this and can also lend a great deal of energy to any magickal work done in conjunction with this ritual and the Asmodai in general.

For those who enjoy the practice of prayer or oration, the following may be useful and can also be used during targeted operations for manifested results.

Oration for Amducias

Anointed one, bringer of destruction, lord of desolation, lay waste to this which no longer serves me. Make barren the works of those who oppose me. Great Amducias, Lord of the void, bring me vindication.

Oration for Asmodeus

Hail great serpent of lust, Asmodeus, thou art sacred. From the flames arise in want, probing deftly into the depths of the abyss. Arise, arise Daemonic

Fire, resplendent in the beauty of your invulnerable flame.

Oration for Asmoday

Blessed is Asmoday, bringer of success and wealth to this world. Bestow your abundance upon me that I may live in comfort and dominion the rest of my days.

Oration for the Asmodai

Glory be to the Asmodai, beloved desire, rise within me that I may have great power over all that stands before me. Through you I am master of my life, my world. Hail to the Asmodai.

Next Steps

Now that you have attuned yourself to the current, what do you do with it? You apply it to your goals, of course. Attuning oneself to the desire/passion current is useless unless you plan on applying it. If you don't, you're merely torturing yourself. This is why working with the Asmodai is great for creative types to destroy creative blocks of all sorts. You can most definitely attach your own magickal rites to this one, including scrying so that you may speak with the Asmodai and seek advice on a plethora of matters. From work, to relationships, to spiritual contentment, if there's desire or passion behind it, the Asmodai can be of great benefit.

Modifications

All rituals can be modified to bring the magician
his/her desired results. Modification can also be
helpful during injury and illness or during periods
where a full-blown ritual is impractical (such as
visiting the Catholic in-laws). This ritual can be
done entirely in the astral temple if necessary. Tea
lights can be used in place of candles. An incense
composed of a pinch of saffron, one teaspoon of
cinnamon, one teaspoon of sandalwood, and a half
cup of red or yellow rose petals may be burned
during this ritual. As this is a Fire Rite, this work
can be done in front of a fire pit with the seals set
out in a row next to it. The magician should be
facing south in this instance.

Rite of Zagan

Rite of Zagan is one of the more notorious rituals of the Demonolatry tradition. It is designed to turn situations into their opposites, just like the Daemon Zagan is purported to do. Generally, this ritual is considered a Keeper Rite, a ritual only shared when a person has a dire need for it, but the problem therein is that many people need real transformation. Because of that, and because I don't believe in 'secret' or 'hidden' knowledge, I have chosen to share this ritual with all of you. This Rite has successfully been used by people from all walks of life to do everything from assisting in sobriety, to losing weight, and more. Deeper spiritual changes are also possible with Zagan. This might include things such combating fears (like fear of success or failure) and helping a person with low self-esteem find a higher self-worth.

This, like a lot of magick, works on the magician's psyche. Because of this, one of the most important things you need to define before performing this ritual is what you want to change and why. A clear goal with a realistic assessment is key to the rite's success. By clearly defining the desired outcome, and I contend this is true for any magickal operation, we firmly set our intent in our psyches. When we do that, we become more aware of changes that need to be made and the opportunities that present themselves to make those changes possible.

Why not just a spell instead of an entire rite? The preparation and process of the rite, the psychodrama of the ritual itself, goes a long way to establishing intent. And as we all know, in magick, intent is everything. It determines whether or not the outcome of a spell or ritual will be failure, moderate success, or complete success. For those of you who do not need excessive psychodrama to establish your intent, as some people are naturally more focused and need less to affect chance, you should feel free to cut the excess or unnecessary parts of the ritual (like the balancing elemental circle) and stick to the creation of the Zagan magickal artifact described in the body of the ritual – effectively turning it into more simple spell work.

If for some reason the creation of the artifact itself does not work for you, consider starting over and re-doing the entire ritual.

Preliminary Preparation: Some people may choose to bathe and cleanse themselves with sage oil or smoke before performing any ritual. If you suffer from any psychological distress, including depression or anxiety, this is always a good idea. It assures you don't take as much negativity into the ritual with you. You might also drink a full glass of water, blessed by Leviathan if you so choose, before performing the operation as it is symbolic of internal cleansing.

What You Need:
- 1 Green Candle leaning more to the yellowish side of the green spectrum to spark creative solutions and promote acceptance and excitement about a new change. Not surprisingly, Zagan is an Earth element whose ruling planet is the Sun. So, while yellow would work great as well, the green tone adds more in the way of mood. Color psychology is a very important aspect of magick.
- 1 Wood or clay disk and something to carve or engrave it with. If you use paint, use gold. If you can afford a gold-colored disk and have tools to engrave metal, that would work, too. If you want to use stone, try Aventurine, Topaz, or Amber. All are ruled by the Sun and would enhance Zagan's influence.
- 1 Sigil of Zagan printed or drawn on a piece of paper.

If you are performing the full ritual, you will also want a ritual dagger, plain white candles for each quadrant of the ritual space, a piece of parchment, magical ink and a quill, a lancet device, and a bowl to burn the final request.

Place the altar at the Southwest quadrant of the ritual space. This ritual assumes west is Earth and places Water north.

This ritual may be done skyclad or robed. Use the following Enns (or Daemonic invocations) to gather the elemental Daemons at their compass points of your ritual space. Feel free to use elemental spirits of the Goetia if you are uncomfortable with the following. (See Daemonolatry Goetia for more.) Always remember that the reason for this is to promote balance within the ritual space and balance within the magician for the magickal work. Not everyone will want to use an elementally balanced ritual space to work. But I recommend it for beginners. More advanced practitioners may choose to invoke Daemons more congruent to the purpose of change, or to their specific situation.

To invoke, go to each elemental point in the room and recite the following enns while tracing a Z and D shape in the air in front of you. (For more about this, see *The Complete Book of Demonolatry*)

Since this is a ritual of new beginning, start at the west (Earth), north (Water), east (Air), and south (Fire).
- To Invoke Earth: Lirach Tasa Vefa Wehlic, Belial.
- To Invoke Water: Jedan Tasa hoet naca, Leviathan.

• To Invoke Air: Renich Tasa Uberaca Biasa Icar, Lucifer.
• To Invoke Fire: Ganic Tasa fubin, Flereous.

For those of you new to this method, I think it will become rather clear why we've placed the altar in the Southwest quadrant.

From the center of the ritual space, you will want to invoke Zagan using the enn: *Anay on ca secore Zagan tasa.*

Now, carve your name into the green candle, then ZAGAN. If you are into oils and incenses, you can dress the candle with a Zagan oil and burn a Zagan incense, but these steps are optional.

NOTE: If you want to make your own Zagan incense or oil, try the following recipe: 1 teaspoon Storax, 1 teaspoon crushed Frankincense, 2 tablespoons of Oak Moss (If you're looking for a more solar aspect - more Sorath-like - try adding 2 tablespoons Calamus Root, and 1 tablespoon of crushed Cinquefoil to your teaspoon of Storax). For the oil, add this to ½ cup Grapeseed oil. For incense, burn it alone.

Light the candle. Now, take your sigil of Zagan:

Continue chanting Zagan's enn while you carve or paint the sigil onto your wood, metal, or clay disk, or the stone. Whatever you've chosen. (If you want to get more creative here and drill a hole in your chosen item so you can wear it as a pendant, that's fine.)

When finished, hold the newly created magickal item in your hands and focus on your INTENT. What is it you want to change? Why? How can you get there? For some of you, especially mediums, you may end up getting some Daemonic input here.

You may anoint the sigil with the oil if you have decided to make it. Again, this is an optional step.

Next, on the paper or parchment on the altar, state exactly what you want to happen. Sign your name to this. Draw the seal of Zagan on the paper, then lancet your finger and apply 1-3 drops of your blood on the paper. Now read what you've written aloud. (If you need to be quiet you can do this in your head.) Fold the paper up, set flame to it from the green candle, and drop it into the offering/burning bowl until it is just ash.

Now, spend some time quietly reflecting about your situation and the change you want to make.

Imagine yourself as the changed person you want
to be. Envision yourself having everything you
want. Do this until you feel as though you have
already achieved what you want.

Then rise, thank Zagan and ask him to be present in
your life until the change is complete. (We do not
use a license to depart because we want the
Daemonic influence to stick around.) Then thank
any other Daemons you've invoked during the ritual
and tell them to go in peace. It would sound like:

*Thank you, Lord/Lady (insert Daemon name here),
for being present during this rite. Go in peace.*

Extinguish all but the altar candle (which you
should burn at least an hour), take up your new
magickal sigil, and you are welcome to leave the
ritual space with it. Carry your sigil with you from
the ritual until the change you seek has been
achieved.

To dispose of the ashes of the request, take them
outside and let the wind carry them off.

Continue burning the candle nightly during
meditation on your situation until it is completely
extinguished. I recommend using a 10-inch taper
and doing a nightly meditation for a week after
performing the ritual.

The meditation and visualization are important parts of this ritual.

Further Considerations: Feel free to write your own invocations and make them as flowery or simple as you wish. Also, you can perform this ritual in the astral temple if performing it physically is an issue for whatever reason. However – the actual sigil artifact is significant and should therefore be created in the real world. Obviously turning the sigil into a pendant is going to be the easiest way to carry it with you. Otherwise, just carry it in your left pocket and don't forget it or accidentally run it through the laundry.

As with all rituals and spells, the more you personalize it and the more you modify it for your needs, the more powerful it is. Feel free to experiment.

Now to the final bit of advice about this ritual. Don't panic if it seems your life is turned upside down and suddenly has more problems than it did before. Sometimes, for meaningful change to occur, the old, comfortable stalemate you're stuck in has to be destroyed! This may mean that bad or hurtful relationships may suddenly end, you may get unexpected news, you could lose your job (or gain one), etc. Remember that Zagan turns things into their opposite. If the change you're expecting is big, expect big, possibly jolting changes. If you aren't prepared for that, or willing to accept that, do not perform this rite. You need to want the change at any cost. Especially if you know it's good for you.

I leave you with this: Accept responsibility for all of your magick and remember that all magick has consequences. Results may vary due to individual work-ethic.

Sledgehammer Daemons

I often get the question when Zagan should be utilized in ritual work to manifest meaningful change. I was even asked recently if someone should do a Zagan Rite for a couple trying to get pregnant.

So first — before you jump on the Zagan bandwagon pause, assess, and think of all the pros and cons of working with a Daemon like Zagan before rushing into the temple to change you or someone else's life.

First things first – Zagan is one of the Daemons that turns something into its opposite. So, if you're broke and unemployed, and that seems to be your natural setting, Zagan might be a good choice. However, if this is simply a temporary situation, a less forceful Daemon like Belphegor or Belial might do the trick. Think of it this way — are you trying to take down a wall, pound in a nail, or push in a tack? Would you take a sledgehammer to a tack? For most people, the answer is no. Tacks only require a little force, whereas a nail may need more force to get them in. To take down a wall, however, it's all about knowing what is necessary, the resources you have in your toolbox, and working with the right tool for the job.

Think of Zagan's influence as a sledgehammer. I

would apply his influence sparingly, and only in cases where things need to change (i.e., you need to knock down a wall). So, for example, if you constantly find yourself broke and unable to hold a job – you really need to get your life together – go ahead and call Zagan. But if you're rarely unemployed and you don't usually experience financial hardship, save Zagan's influence for something else.

The same thing applies when you're doing work for others. If you want to help some happy newlyweds get pregnant, consider kinder, gentler Daemonic influence to help them conceive. Don't bring in a sledgehammer to put a nail in the wall for a picture. You'll put a hole in the wall, and you could inadvertently destroy the relationship of the happy couple without meaning to.

Some other good reasons to call in Zagan:
- You want to overcome a self-destructive addiction.
- You need to change your life before you end up hurting yourself or others.
- You are crippling yourself or drowning in your own ineptitude.

Those are all great reasons to pull out the sledgehammer, take down the wall, and rebuild with something that better serves you.

See – Zagan has this tendency to take a person's life and flip it upside down. This is usually not a pleasant or peaceful process. There could potentially be a lot of pain, suffering, and fear involved. The point being that sometimes you have to tear everything down to the foundation in order to rebuild it into something better. But sometimes you don't need that. You have to develop discernment and wisdom to know when to tear something down, or just to apply a little force.

There are other Daemons out there like Zagan. Ones that I don't recommend practitioners work with without thorough consideration unless they don't mind the 2×4 of reality knocking them upside the head. Don't get me wrong – I get it – sometimes we all need some tough love, just make sure you're choosing the right-sized hammer for the job. Do you want your hopes and dreams crushed by reality? Do you mind losing certain things you love in order to get better things? These are the kinds of questions only YOU can answer for yourself.

Other hard hitting Daemonic forces you should be mindful of working with include:

Sorath – Sorath will make you face ALL of the fears holding you back, including some you didn't even know you had. Sorath also tends to test one's time management skills, communication skills, business sense, and skill overall just to see if you can hack it.

Especially if you're working with him to take your career to a new level. He also tends to bring up the past and things you may not be so proud of – making you deal with them, and that's never fun.

Claunek – While Claunek may be relatively tame for some folks (hey – a lot of folks love Claunek) – for some people (those who are paying attention at least), he's going to point out all your weaknesses (including skills, character flaws etc....) and make you face the facts about your career/job/etc. This can be extremely painful when it comes to making you face dream crushing realities. At that point, of course, it's up to you whether or not you listen to what he's telling you. He'll highlight your problem areas — it's up to you to fix them. Otherwise, you'll just end up in the same place you were before you worked with him. (Pathworking Hint: If you keep finding yourself in the same situation over and over again, it's you.)

Thoth – Oh, harmless Thoth. You're probably wondering why I added him to the list. Well, again, any magician actually paying attention when they work with Thoth will be forced to up their game at whatever outcome they're seeking (especially if you're seeking to improve a skill). Thoth doesn't tolerate laziness, irresponsibility, or half-assed anything. If you want to learn, for example, to be a more effective magician (as Thoth can help with that) – you better be serious, and you better not be

a lazy, half-assed student. He will metaphorically shine a light on all your mistakes, flaws, and shortcomings, then force you to practice over and over again until you eventually improve. Or he'll subject you to scathing criticism from your peers. People generally have one of two reactions from this. They either reassess, self-edit, practice and improve, or they drop it like a hot rock and cower in a cave of self-loathing somewhere. I've watched that happen to a few folks over the years. Ouch.
There are a few others, but those are some of the heavier hitters.

Will every magician experience these same things with these Daemons? No. Of course not. A magician's personality, their ability for self-assessment and self-improvement, their relationship with the Daemonic force in question (and how they harmonize with that force), their coping skills, and the person's actual life situation and goals will all play a heavy role in HOW the magickal operation manifests and how hard-hitting the Daemon actually is.

Also note that if you have a life jarring experience with one of these Daemons – that doesn't make you a bad magician unless you don't grow and change as a result. Just like people who have never had a life jarring experience with a Daemon are not better magicians. Actually – people who have great experiences with every Daemon they run across likely aren't doing the self-work and self-assessment required to grow as a person.

My goal in sharing this article isn't to ward anyone away from working with these Daemons. Just to encourage you to stop and think before running into the temple to summon a sledgehammer for your tack (or nail) of a problem.

Orobas vs. Ouroboros

This comes up every time I teach this class. Is Orobas the same as the Egyptian Ouroboros? They have the same enn, after all.

This often depends on who you talk to, because Orobas can teach us the nature of the divine and the universe and Ouroboros represents the never-ending cycle of life, death, and rebirth. The snake that eats its own tail. The beginning and the end. A symbol of fertility.

Both are Watery spirits. Both symbolize wisdom. I say that Orobas is a tamer version of Leviathan in the sense that the emotional tides with Orobas are gentler, but that is perhaps because Orobas is inevitable because Orobas is the cyclic nature of the universe. Which is ultimately why he can teach us the nature of such things.

So, in that sense you could say, yes, Orobas and Ouroboros are the same energy, but perhaps different aspects of the same. Perhaps they're twinned. And if so, Orobas would be the passive energy and Ouroboros would be the active energy of the same force.

Ultimately though, I will leave it up to you as to whether or not you view them as the same

Daemonic force, just different aspects. Or perhaps they're the exact same. Or maybe you think they're completely different.

Consider writing down your thoughts about this in your journal.

[Author's Note]: Ultimately someone asks me if I've just "asked the Daemons" about this and what did they say? I have asked about this, and I received the answer: *"All things are the same, just different degrees of the same"* which comes from *The Kybalion.* I tend to take this as a yes, and that I'm on the right track with the idea of different aspects, same energy, active vs. passive.

Conclusion

Thank you for picking up a copy of this book. A lot of people take this course hoping to learn about the Goetic spirits and end up learning so much more. It is my hope that you leave this work feeling more connected, and stronger in your skills as a magician in both low and high magick.

Remember that nothing in this book should be treated as gospel. Instead, think of everything herein as mere suggestions for the work. Carve your own path.

May the Daemonic Divine forever burn brightly within you. You are a divine spark.

Made in United States
Orlando, FL
29 April 2025

60879763R00216